Professional Knowledge, Professional Lives

Professional Learning

Series Editors: Ivor Goodson and Andy Hargreaves

The work of teachers has changed significantly in recent years and now, more than ever, there is a pressing need for high quality professional development. This timely new series examines the actual and possible forms of professional learning, professional knowledge, professional development and professional standards that are beginning to emerge and be debated at the beginning of the twenty-first century. The series will be important reading for teachers, teacher educators, staff developers and policy makers throughout the English-speaking world.

Published and forthcoming titles:

Ivor Goodson: *Professional Knowledge, Professional Lives*
Andy Hargreaves: *Teaching in the Knowledge Society*
Alma Harris: *Improving Schools through Teacher Leadership*
Garry Hoban: *Teacher Learning for Educational Change*
Bob Lingard, Debra Hayes, Martin Mills and Pam Christie: *Leading Learning*
Judyth Sachs: *The Activist Teaching Profession*

Professional Knowledge,
Professional Lives
Studies in education and change

Ivor F Goodson

Open University Press
Maidenhead · Philadelphia

Open University Press
McGraw-Hill Education
McGraw-Hill House
Shoppenhangers Road
Maidenhead
Berkshire
England
SL6 2QL

email: enquiries@openup.co.uk
world wide web: www.openup.co.uk

and

325 Chestnut Street
Philadelphia, PA 19106, USA

First published 2003

A catalogue record of this book is available from the British Library

ISBN 0 335 20411 2 (pb)   0 335 20412 0 (hb)

Library of Congress Cataloging-in-Publication Data
CIP data has been applied for

Typeset by RefineCatch Limited, Bungay, Suffolk
Printed in Great Britain by Bell and Bain Ltd, Glasgow

Why are you watching?
Somebody has to . . .

Franz Kafka

Contents

Series editors' preface

Teaching today is increasingly complex work, requiring the highest standards of professional practice to perform it well (Goodson and Hargreaves 1996). It is the core profession, the key agent of change in today's knowledge society. Teachers are the midwives of that knowledge society. Without them, or their competence, the future will be malformed and stillborn. In the United States, George W. Bush's educational slogan has been to leave no child behind. What is clear today in general, and in this book in particular, is that leaving no child behind means leaving no teacher or leader behind either. Yet, teaching too is also in crisis, staring tragedy in the face. There is a demographic exodus occurring in the profession as many teachers in the ageing cohort of the Boomer generation are retiring early because of stress, burnout or disillusionment with the impact of years of mandated reform on their lives and work. After a decade of relentless reform in a climate of shaming and blaming teachers for perpetuating poor standards, the attractiveness of teaching as a profession has faded fast among potential new recruits.

Teaching has to compete much harder against other professions for high calibre candidates than it did in the last period of mass recruitment – when able women were led to feel that only nursing and secretarial work were viable options. Teaching may not yet have reverted to being an occupation for 'unmarriageable women and unsaleable men' as Willard Waller described it in 1932, but many American inner cities now run their school systems on high numbers of uncertified teachers. The teacher recruitment crisis in England has led some schools to move to a four-day week; more and more schools are run on the increasingly casualized labour of temporary teachers from overseas, or endless supply teachers whose quality busy administrators do not always have time to monitor (Townsend 2001).

Meanwhile in the Canadian province of Ontario, in 2001, hard-nosed and hard-headed reform strategies led in a single year to a decrease in applications to teacher education programmes in faculties of education by 20–25 per cent, and a drop in a whole grade level of accepted applicants.

Amid all this despair and danger though, there remains great hope and some reasons for optimism about a future of learning that is tied in its vision to an empowering, imaginative and inclusive vision for teaching as well. The educational standards movement is showing visible signs of overreaching itself as people are starting to complain about teacher shortages in schools, and the loss of creativity and inspiration in classrooms (Hargreaves *et al.* 2001). There is growing international support for the resumption of more humane middle years' philosophies in the early years of secondary school that put priority on community and engagement, alongside curriculum content and academic achievement. School districts in the United States are increasingly seeing that high quality professional development for teachers is absolutely indispensable to bringing about deep changes in student achievement (Fullan 2001). In England and Wales, policy documents and White Papers are similarly advocating for more 'earned autonomy', and freedom from curriculum constraints and inspection requirements, where schools and teachers are performing well (e.g. DfES 2001). Governments almost everywhere are beginning to speak more positively about teachers and teaching – bestowing honour and respect where blame and contempt had prevailed in the recent past.

The time has rarely been more opportune or more pressing to think more deeply about what professional learning, professional knowledge and professional status should look like for the new generation of teachers who will shape the next three decades of public education. Should professional learning accompany increased autonomy for teachers, or should its provision be linked to the evidence of demonstrated improvements in pupil achievement results? Do successful schools do better when the professional learning is self-guided, discretionary and intellectually challenging, while failing schools or schools in trouble benefit from required training in the skills that evidence shows can raise classroom achievement quickly? And does accommodating professional learning to the needs of different schools and their staffs constitute administrative sensitivity and flexibility (Hopkins *et al.* 1997), or a kind of professional development apartheid (Hargreaves, forthcoming)? These are the kinds of questions and issues which this series on professional learning sets out to address.

References

DfES (Department for Education and Skills) (2001) *Achieving Success*. London, HMSO.

Fullan, M. (2001) *Leading in a Culture of Change*. San Francisco: Jossey-Bass/Wiley.

Goodson, I. and Hargreaves, A. (eds), *Teachers' Professional Lives*, New York: Falmer Press.

Hargreaves, A. (forthcoming) *Teaching in the Knowledge Society*. New York: Teachers College Press.

Hargreaves, A., Earl, L., Moore, S. and Manning, S. (2001) *Learning to Change: Beyond teaching subjects and standards*. San Francisco: Jossey-Bass/Wiley.

Hopkins, D., Harris, A. and Jackson, D. (1997) Understanding the schools capacity for development: Growth states and strategies, *School Leadership and Management*, 17(3): 401–11.

Townsend, J. (2001) It's bad – trust me, I teach there, *Sunday Times*, 2 December.

Waller, W. (1932) *The Sociology of Teaching*. New York: Russell & Russell.

Preface

This book is concerned with forms of professional knowledge and the relationships of such knowledge to our understandings of educational change. In the initial chapters, the current situation of professional knowledge is scrutinized with particular regard to the location of educational study in the faculties of education. The fate of disciplinary patterns of study, which have come under great attack from the proponents of more practical perspectives, will be examined.

Practical perspectives promoted by a wide spectrum of advocates have become part of a fashionable discourse around teacher education and educational study. In the past decade, some of the results of such practical fundamentalism are held up for scrutiny. The particular relationship, which is set up for investigation later in the book, is the relationship between patterns of professional knowledge and educational change, and the need for a revivified form of teacher professionalism.

The relationship between advocates of practical perspectives and teacher professionalism is currently one that has not been systematically analysed and yet, within it, there are the seeds of considerable ambivalence and antipathy. Confining professional knowledge entirely within the practical terrain would not seem a well-thought out strategy for raising general professional standards. A much wider conception of professional knowledge would need to be defined and advocated.

Hence the argument is developed that a more active notion of teachers' professional knowledge can be explored and consolidated by work which focuses on the 'teacher's life and work' using more reflexive and action research-based modes. From the first, it should be stressed that these are not presented as a final package of new research modes, rather as some examples, some early indicators – the 'green shoots' of a revivified pattern of educational elaboration. While a broader conception of professional knowledge and professional development is a worthwhile end in itself, there are further benefits from a wider focus on professional life and work in terms of the elaboration and delivery of educational reform and change initiatives.

The second half of the book explores the link between work of this kind and new change initiatives and change theories. The growing understanding of teachers' beliefs, motivations and missions provides a new way of exploring some of the misconceptions and misapplications that can be found at the heart of some of the new initiatives aimed at restructuring our schools. Working from longitudinal studies of school reform in the United States and Canada, as well as the United Kingdom, the role of personal beliefs and missions can be fruitfully explored. As has been slowly understood by policy makers, it is difficult to deliver successful change without the involvement and enthusiasm of teachers. In the early stages, optimistic reformers often try to deliver school change almost *in spite of* the teachers' beliefs and missions. Such brutal restructuring is never likely to work.

The starting point has to be a fine-tuned understanding of the motives and missions that teachers bring to their work. These must constitute part of the 'negotiations' with reform personnel that constitute meaningful change processes. To undertake reform in ignorance or defiance of teachers' beliefs and missions is a high-cost, high-risk strategy likely to end with low delivery. As politically attractive 'symbolic action' it has some short-term potential for convincing 'publics' of governmental intention. In the medium term and long term, it is far more problematic as evidence accumulates of non-delivery of change objectives, or of the 'massaging' of figures to create the impression that change has been delivered.

Summary of each chapter

Part one

Chapter 1: Introduction: Forms of professional knowledge

In this introductory chapter, the state of professional knowledge with regard to teaching and teacher education over the past decade or so will be reviewed. The link between patterns of knowledge and different versions of teacher professionalism will be established to set the scenes for a closer investigation of these matters in the following chapters. The centrality of bodies of knowledge to the claim to professional status in Western societies is reviewed and established.

Chapter 2: Education as a practical matter
This chapter looks at the arguments, deployed in a range of statements and agencies within the United Kingdom, which promote the notion of practical knowledge as the central form of knowledge for teachers. While this essay was written in the mid-1990s, and precedes the new Labour government elected in 1997, little has changed in terms of the trajectory of government policy although the ongoing displacement of disciplinary study has accelerated. There has, it is true, been some softening of 'rhetoric', but little evidence that the elevation of practice over theory has been replaced by partnership even in some of the more evidence-based modalities. For this reason, I have let the original intention of this essay remain and therefore the practical perspective is closely interrogated, and then a variety of critiques to this position are presented.

Chapter 3: Representing teachers: bringing teachers back in
This chapter scrutinizes the growing movement to work with teachers' stories and narratives as part of a desire to develop the teacher's practical knowledge. At precisely the time that teachers' voices are being enthusiastically pursued and promoted, teachers' work is being technicized and narrowed. As the movement grows to celebrate the teacher's knowledge, it is becoming less and less promising as a focus of research and reflection. The teacher's work intensifies as more and more central edicts and demands impinge on the teacher's world, leaving the space for reflection and research progressively squeezed. Stories and narratives, therefore, can form an unintended coalition with those forces which would divorce the teacher from knowledge of political and micro-political perspectives, from theory and from broader cognitive maps of influence and power. Hence new modalities, using teachers' stories and narratives as a starting point, need to embrace wider historical and political discourses.

Chapter 4: The story so far: personal knowledge and the political
In this chapter, written in 1994, the use of story genres is reviewed in its wider social context. The use of 'storying' as a technique is now common in the media and, as a result, has begun to take on a normative characteristic. In general, this chapter is concerned with exploring how storytelling genres, as well as being used to democratize and extend our understandings, can be used to narrow and trivialize them. Examples are provided from studies of the media to show how storytelling can become part of a 'dumbing down' process. It is then argued that we need to be alert to these dangers in the use of storytelling genres within educational research. The kind of antidote to this danger which is presented is the extension of 'a story of action into a theory of context'. The move from life story to life history provides us with a way of presenting stories in a wider context, thereby avoiding the dangers of narrowness and trivialization.

Chapter 5: Developing life and work histories of teachers
In this chapter, the justifications for using life history work in the study of teachers are presented in detail. A range of rationales are defined and argued for. In addition, a good deal of contextual and thematic data is presented to show how life history work can help us explore some of the major issues underlying the teacher's work. In particular, we show how life history work can transform our understandings of particular issues, such as teacher 'burn out' and teacher 'drop out'. When viewed from a managerial perspective, these issues can be presented in one particular light, but when examined using life history work, a different perspective is developed and a whole different set of understandings generated.

Part two

Chapter 6: Introduction: Studying educational change
This chapter introduces the theme of educational change. Existing change theories are scrutinized and it is argued that they are historically inadequate and parsimonious with regard to understandings of teachers' beliefs and missions. Work employing a life history approach can provide important new insights in the domain of teachers' understandings.

Chapter 7: The personality of change
This chapter develops from the longitudinal Spencer study, 'Change over Time', in North American schools. Personal change needs to be accorded a more substantial role in the development of educational change theory. Here a case study provides evidence of the 'personality of change' – the role of personal beliefs and missions in educational practice.

Chapter 8: Personal missions and professional development
This chapter extends the analysis of personal beliefs and missions within the educational change process. Sections are provided on organizational memory, mentoring and the key questions of retention and recruitment. Here the lacuna, with regard to personal perspectives, is shown to be a major flaw in change and reform initiatives and theories.

Chapter 9: Social histories of educational change
This chapter reviews educational change theories and modalities, locating them in historical periods within the second half of the twentieth century. New models of change are developed and prospects for change reviewed.

Chapter 10: The educational researcher as a public intellectual
In this chapter, the relationship between public intellectual work and educational study is explored. The chapter originated as the Lawrence

Stenhouse Memorial Lecture given to the British Educational Research Association Conference in York in 1997. The crisis of positionality, with regard to the changing patterns within teacher education, is defined through a historical case study of the fate of teacher education study in the period from the 1960s onwards (a case study of the Centre for Applied Research in Education is deployed to provide a grounded evidence of this change). The final section and the next chapter look towards the future and towards a new moral order for schooling.

Chapter 11: Educational change and the crisis of professionalism (with Andy Hargreaves)

In the final chapter, the implications of the status of professional knowledge for teachers' professional standing are explored. The link which is established is that in order for teachers to continue to be viewed as professionals, they have to both own 'a body of professional knowledge' and explore the moral dimensions of teaching as a craft. A good deal of the current changes in education challenge the status of teachers' professional knowledge and, in doing so, threaten to undercut teachers' professionalism. This is of profound importance for the future of teaching and, in particular, for the moral basis on which the craft of teaching operates.

As can be seen, the chapters in the book follow a particular line of argument and inquiry with respect to professional knowledge and educational study, which is perhaps worth reiterating as follows.

The first and earliest section considers the dilemmas of disciplinary knowledge as applied to practical milieux. Some of these dilemmas are confronted and the deficits of disciplinary knowledge analysed, but the full flight to 'practical fundamentalism' is resisted. New genres of professional knowledge and research are, it is conceded, required, but specifically not ones which evacuate completely the theoretical and contextual domain. This is to throw the baby out with the disciplinary bathwater.

In the middle section, the new genres of teacher narratives and stories are considered. Their potential to connect in new ways is noted, but so too is the seeming abdication of contextual and theoretical concerns.

What is required, as the last section seeks to illustrate, is professional knowledge that welcomes the new forms of connectedness, but explores the contextual parameters and theoretical implications of school practices. Here we are on new ground and a number of examples are provided to indicate how these modalities might merge and provide new and generative ways forward.

Acknowledgements

My thanks to the Spencer Foundation for funding a good deal of the work reported in these pages. They are a model research and funding agency to work with – always prompt in response and articulate in terms of their own needs for accountability and reportage.

Particular thanks to my two research team members, Martha Foote and Michael Baker. Their conscientiousness and integrity have been a feature of the research throughout and I thank them both sincerely. Also, thanks to the other team members at the University of Toronto: Dean Fink, Carol Beynon and Corrie Giles. And most of all, I have enjoyed my sparring contest with Andy Hargreaves and his faithful deputy, Shawn Moore!

Particular and special thanks to Nicky Skivington for her enduring professionalism in handling this manuscript – she has always been a pleasure to work with.

'Education as a practical matter', by I. Goodson, first appeared in the *Cambridge Journal of Education*, 25(2): 137–48, 1995 (reproduced with permission by Taylor & Francis: http://www.tandf.co.uk).

'Representing teachers: bringing teachers back in', by I. Goodson, first appeared in *Teaching and Teaching Education*, 13(1): 111–17, 1995 (reproduced with permission by Elsevier Science).

'The story so far: personal knowledge and the political', by I. Goodson, first appeared in the *Journal of Qualitative Studies in Education*, 8(1): 89–98, 1995 (reproduced with permission by Taylor & Francis: http://www.tandf.co.uk).

'Social histories of educational change' is based upon the article which appeared in the *Journal of Educational Change*, 2(1): 45–63, 2002 (reproduced with permission from the editor of the journal, Kluwer Academic Publishers).

'The educational researcher as a public intellectual', by I. Goodson, was published in the *British Educational Research Journal*, 25(3): 277–97, 1999 (reproduced with permission from the editor of the journal, Carfax Publishing).

'Educational change and the crisis of professionalism', by I. Goodson (with Andy Hargreaves), first appeared as the article 'The principled professional' in *Prospects: Professionalism in Teaching*, XXX(2): 181–8, ©UNESCO 2000 (reproduced by permission of UNESCO).

The cartoon by Steve Bell, 'Reforming the NHS', appeared in the *Guardian* on 6 March 1996 and is reproduced with permission by Steve Bell.

Part 1

one

Introduction: Forms of professional knowledge

The forms of knowledge that we produce and use are often closely related to perceptions that we have of ourselves and the projections of ourselves that we undertake. As we shall see, this is of great importance with regard to teachers' professional knowledge.

As a way of personal introduction (but also in order to develop a more general point), let me provide an historical example of the way that forms of knowledge are implicated in the process of self-building by retrospectively creating some of the forms of knowledge that were employed in those working-class communities in which I grew up. One of the key forms of knowledge that was employed in my community upbringing was story-telling, so let me stay with that tradition and tell a story to underline the argument that I am trying to make.

Every Christmas in my community, families and wider kinship networks would gather on Christmas Day to party, get drunk and interact on a variety of levels. In the afternoon on Christmas Day, two or three hours were set aside for community time. Normally, a major part of the time was taken up by the telling of jokes (often of the most appallingly racist and sexist kind, it should be said). In addition, there would be other acts, such as my Uncle George playing the saw and my Uncle Clay playing the spoons. But the stories which were treated with the most systematic attention and concentration were two stories that were told every Christmas by my father. Such was the reverence with which these stories were received that I, as a child, knew that some important statement was being made about us as a community. The form of knowledge which was purveyed and engaged with, defined us as a group.

The two stories were these. First there was the story of my Aunt Hilda.

Like all of my father's sisters (he had 12), she worked in domestic service for one of the rich manor house owners in the area. As it happened (or so the story went), she was rather beautiful and at some point in her domestic service career had an affair with the 'squire', the owner of the manor house. Unfortunately she became pregnant and seven months into her pregnancy was found drowned in the river near the manor house. This story was always received in a fresh way, in stunned silence, but with a sense of collective outrage. The story was told in a way that made it a form of social interrogation of the class structure which brought forth this result.

The second story was even more pertinent. My granddad had become ill at home and had to be pushed on a handbarrow to the local village hospital. Unfortunately he was denied access to the hospital and had to be pushed another seven miles to the local workhouse, where the poor were incarcerated when ill. He died that night. To die in the 'workhouse' was a particular destiny, a particularly feared end for the working class and again, in telling this story, my father ranged far and wide in his commentary on the social structure. The story form carried a deep theoretical structure immanent within.

The point I am making is that the forms of knowledge that were presented in this family gathering were of a wide range. But the forms of knowledge, which clearly were held and received with reverence, were those which allowed a community to present cultural commentaries and theories. In doing so, they clearly sensed that the form of knowledge they held in this kind of storytelling was of an empowering and substantial kind. By having these forms of knowledge and by creating these forms of discourse, it was a matter of community consciousness that we were a different people that could think for ourselves. The knowledge we had defined the people we were.

Likewise, the forms of knowledge which teachers have are substantially implicated in the kind of people teachers are and believe themselves to be. At the moment, as I will argue later in the chapter, those forms of knowledge are being substantially restructured and, as a result, are substantially changing the kind of people that teachers are and are seen to be.

In the first section of this book I look in some detail at the effect of the embrace of 'practice' as a fundamentalist mantra defining forms of professional knowledge and professionalism. Later I address some of the implications for academic/professional discourses and policies of newer postmodernist developments, particularly the 'politics of difference'. In the world of teacher education, this is playing out in the emergence and ongoing construction of a set of balkanized discourses and knowledge. These developments seem to fit well with a broader matrix of emergent patterns of governance in education.

At a time when rampant globalization is rewriting the world and doing so in a deafening and often unitary voice, teachers and other academic groups are not responding with any sort of unitary professional voice. We appear to be mostly concerned to respond by embracing a cacophony of distinct and different voices. By responding in this way, we face a somewhat acute humanistic paradox. In short, we may be in danger of disempowering the professional at the same time as we empower more distinct, diverse and long-silenced voices. On this analysis, it is possible to see unitary global culture and emerging postmodernist discourses as compatible companions, postmodernism being the cultural apparatus which accompanies a culminating phase of globalizing corporate power.

A particular problem in all this, I believe, is posed by those genres which, often for the best of reasons, have sought to sponsor new voices – the world of 'stories', 'narratives' and 'lives'. All of this work is vitally important, but as currently constructed, these genres tend to lead us away from context and theorizing, away from the conceptualizing of power.

As a result, some work in the area of teachers' lives has begun to explore a more contextualizing and theorizing aspect – what might be called, drawing from Lawrence Stenhouse (1976: 7), 'the story of action within a theory of context'. In the dialectical development of theories of contextualities, the possibility exists to link our 'stories', 'narratives' and 'lives' to wider patterns of structuration and social organization. So the focus on theories of context is, in fact, an attempt to answer the critique that listening to lives and narrating them valorizes the subjectivity of the powerless individual. In the act of ostensibly 'giving voice', we may be 'silencing' in another way, silencing because, in fact, we teachers and researchers have given up the concern to 'theorize' context.

I suspect we have done this: certainly, I believe, this is true of most egalitarian scholars, because of the fear of colonizing and coopting the exploited and powerless – in this case, teachers. But I think we let our good emotions run too far, not least because they silence *us*, as well as narrow the teachers' voices towards a more quiescent narrative. Sandra Harding argues

> for the scientific and epistemological advantage of starting from the lives of those who have been devalued, neglected, excluded from the centre of the social order; who generate less interest in ignorance about how the social order works; who provide perspectives from the other side of racial struggles; who enable a different perspective, one from everyday life; who in some cases provide 'outsider within' perspectives; who mediate relations between nature and culture in ways different from those of European American wo(/)men; and whose activities provide particularly illuminating understanding at its moment in History.
>
> (Harding 1991: 211–12)

People's experience should be seen as the starting point of scientific inquiry, but must go beyond the microscopic and anecdotal. Indeed, we need to be aware that people's lived experiences are dialectically linked to the social relations of the society in which these people are located, and that no one – the researchers included – is ever totally outside these relations (Smith 1987). The difficult task of the social scientist then is to explain 'the social organization of the everyday world' (Smith 1987: 91), by starting from the people's location within it. Smith argues that

> locating the knower in the everyday world and constituting our inquiry in terms of the problematic arising from how it is actually organized in a social process, enable us to see the 'micro' and the 'macro' sociological levels in a determinate relation.
>
> (Smith 1987: 99)

This last point is particularly relevant when we consider criticisms of ethnographical research as being non-generalizable. When we use our case studies, people's lived experience, as starting points of larger structural analysis, then the link between the particular and the general becomes part and parcel of our inquiries. Smith makes this point quite clearly in her thought-provoking book, *The Everyday World as Problematic*. The particular 'case presents itself to us rather as a point of entry, the locus of an experiencing subject, or subjects, into a larger social and economic process' (Smith 1987: 57).

Those advocating wholesale evacuation of university-based research in favour of practice-centred teacher–researcher modes have a good deal to answer for in this regard. For the particular, the personal and the practical have been accorded sacred status over the general, the contextual and the theoretical. In the process, university-based research and university schools of education have surrendered many of their claims to expertise and power.

Some advocates of teacher research seem unaware that in linking their movement to critiques of university research they have in fact connived with those who would reduce the teacher's role to that of technician. Shorn of the power of university support, teacher research has become an easy target for those now restructuring schooling. Standing on its own, teacher research is a 'sitting duck' for those who would reduce the teacher to the role of technician.

Cochran-Smith and Lytle, two of the most articulate advocates of teacher research, have noted the strategic deficits that are now only too clear:

> As it is used in the service of more and more agendas and even institutionalized in certain contexts, it is in danger of becoming anything and everything. As we know, however, anything and everything often lead in the end to nothing of consequence or power. It would be

unfortunate if the generative nature of teacher research ended up contributing to either its marginalization and trivialization, on the one hand, or to its subtle co-optation or colonization, on the other.

(Cochran-Smith and Lytle 1999: 17)

They note how powerful new constituencies are now restructuring the schools and, of course, are doing so without much contestation from the university schools of education now living in reduced circumstances. In this specific sense, by sharing the critique of the universities, the teacher–researcher movement has been implicated in the new attacks on the very agents they were sponsoring – the classroom teacher.

> The standards movement – and with it the proliferation of classroom, school, school district, city, state, and national policies – now dominates the agenda regarding instruction, curriculum, assessment, promotion policies, and other aspects of school life. As pressures for school- and classroom-level accountability intensify, research-based whole-school improvement models become increasingly widespread, the concept of best practice guides discussions about student achievement and teacher education, and the authoritative role of outsiders in school improvement becomes the rule rather than the exception.
>
> (Cochrane-Smith and Lytle 1999: 22)

A new concordat is needed between those in schools and in universities concerned with the development of teacher professionalism. This new partnership – in some senses a retrieval of earlier partnerships – might challenge the 'authoritative role of outsiders' and challenge the utilitarianization of teachers and schooling (see Cochran-Smith and Fries 2001).

In developing teachers' professional knowledge, the joining of 'stories of action' to 'theories of context' (Goodson 1994a; Goodson and Sikes 2001) is especially imperative. Without this kind of knowledge, teaching becomes the technical delivery of other people's purposes. Such a mission is unlikely to appeal to the creative and caring people we need to educate our children.

two

Education as a practical matter

There are moments when many of us sense an odd distance
between the ethos of teacher education and lived lives of the
publics to whom we hope the schools can respond. There
are moments when I feel a similar gap between ourselves
and many of the teachers in those schools. I have some of
our normatives in mind, our styles of explanations, our
ways of putting things.

(Greene 1991: 541)

The aim of this chapter is to explore why it is that so much educational research has seldom seemed useful to the teacher. A secondary question is how that irrelevance has been structured and maintained over the years. There are, I think, many factors, but here I focus on three particularly acute problems. First, the role of the older disciplines in studying education. Secondly, the role of faculties of education or schools of education generally.[1] Thirdly, related to the decline of disciplinary study and the crisis in the faculties of education, the dangers implicit in too hasty an embrace of the panacea of more *practical* study of education.

In reviewing the role of faculties of education and educational study generally, I shall be agreeing with the substance of what is now a well-established and sustained critique, but wishing to disagree about the conclusions thereby drawn and the solutions suggested. My concern is to retrieve and reconceptualize the original theoretical missions of educational study, but to do so in ways that are systematically and structurally engaged with the teacher's life and work (Goodson and Sikes 2001).

In fact, the decline of modernism makes this an interesting time to consider these issues, because of the associated decline and, in some cases, collapse of the disciplinary canons on which much educational research has been built. The disciplinary study of education – for example, history of education, philosophy of education, sociology of education, and so on – has always had a shaky purview within the realms of practitional lore. Long before postmodernism, there was a common-sense view among

[1] Names range from Faculty of Education through to School of Education, College of Education and Department of Education. Here we use Faculty of Education as the generic category.

practitioners that the disciplinary study of education was largely irrelevant to their concerns. This problem of the older disciplines arises, in many cases, because those scholars working in disciplinary modes normally develop their first allegiance to their home discipline. While this is not intrinsically or inevitably a problem, it has often had the effect over time of divorcing such scholars from the world of schooling. This problem is exacerbated when those in the disciplines adopt a hands-off posture with regard to schools; added to which, all too often, these scholars have no previous experience within schools.

The strategic difficulty of the argument presented here is itself symptomatic. I argue that the theoretical mission, particularly as represented by disciplinary scholars, has become imperilled. So I begin by seeming to turn against disciplinary scholarship. Many who share this critique have sought to redirect work towards field-based study; the collection of personal stories; the development of practical knowledge (even, in one case, the elision of the two as personal and practical knowledge). But I also want to argue against this interpretation. It would seem that either I am pathologically critical or these are difficult times to defend and reinscribe the theoretical mission!

Broadly stated, my position is that I stand firmly by the theoretical and contextual study of education. I believe that disciplinary scholars have bravely defended this theoretical mission, but that they have become victims of the 'devil's bargain' involved in their location within universities. It was not the theoretical mission that was flawed, rather the terms of its structural location. I also admire those who have sought to build new modes of educational study which try to redirect work back towards teachers and schools. However, in general, I think they have thrown the theoretical baby out with the bathwater. They have courageously re-embraced the schools and practice, but along the way have surrendered their theoretical missions.

We must always remember the central historical point that theory and practice are not inevitably or intrinsically divorced: it is structures and institutionalized missions that have created the more recent divorce. But new structures and institutionalized practices could consummate a new marriage. Historically, the relationship of theory to practice follows a cyclical pattern.

Certainly, histories of the relationship between theory and practice point to wide differentials in the gap between the two. The dichotomy, far from being wide and intractable, seems to be at least partially tractable and highly variable over time. Simon examined the relationship between theory and practice in three periods: 1880–1900, 1920–1940 and 1940–1960. In the first and last periods, he found 'a close relation between theory and practice'. For instance, in the period 1880–1900:

For a whole concatenation of reasons, and from a variety of motives, it was thought that the masses should be educated, or at least schooled – and they were. This whole enterprise was, as it were, powered by an ideology – or theoretical stance – which emphasized the educatability of the normal child, a view underpinned by advances in the field of psychology and physiology relating to human learning.

(Simon 1985: 49)

The point underlined by the quote, and the evidence about this historical period, is that the potential for close relationship or, at the other extreme, no relationship between theory and practice depends on the political conditions of the time, particularly as expressed in the social purposes and missions defined for our public schools.

At the moment, theory and practice are being driven further and further apart, and it is not just school practitioners who have a sense of irrelevance and alienation. The following extract is from a letter written by a new faculty member, in a foundations department of a faculty of education, and illustrates the sharp feelings of isolation and alienation often found within such departments:

A major breakthrough! In a conversation with one of my colleagues the other day, I happened to mention, just in passing, that I was interested in field-based research and teacher development. With a somewhat perplexed look she suggested that I talk to the chairperson of one of the other divisions within the faculty (division – what an appropriate word!). Anyway, I did. And, lo and behold, it was like a door opened to a whole new world – people who speak the same language, and who have similar ideas and perspectives on teacher education and research. Since then, I have received announcements of pertinent upcoming events; been approached by some other faculty members in that division about possible collaboration on some projects; and invited to present a paper as part of the division's regular seminar series on teacher education. It's hard to believe how completely unaware I've been of all that has been going on around me – and the building is not that big, believe me!

(Knowles and Cole 1991)

The young faculty member in the foundations department rapidly escaped to a new position after the experience of seeing just how narrow were the concerns of her department. While none of this adds up to a conclusive proof of irrelevance, one can see, I think, why practitioners in the school might also, over time, come to view this foundations group and their research as irrelevant. Here I am at one with what Schwab said about curriculum research, and think it also applies to a good deal of disciplinary educational research. He said the field of curriculum was 'moribund':

It is unable, by its present methods and principles, to continue its work and contribute significantly to the advancement of education. It requires new principles which will generate a new view of the character and variety of its problems. It requires new methods appropriate to the new budget of problems.

(Schwab 1978: 287)

There are just too many points at which credibility is strained: the manifest allegiance to the host discipline and not to the educational endeavour; the distance, occasionally disdain, in relation to school and teachers; the absence of any experience of school teaching. None of these are, in themselves, insurmountable obstacles to communication: put together they amount to a collapse of credibility.

In short, it is time for discipline-based scholars to re-examine their terrain and to rework their loyalties. As it stands, the dysfunctionality of so much disciplinary study and teaching is a tragedy for the faculties of education. This is true, not least, because so many good proponents of the theoretical mission have been located within foundational disciplines. The theoretical and academic virtuosity of many disciplinary scholars is currently being wasted by the displacement of their concerns and their institutional history. The problem of disciplinary studies is not primarily to do with any absence of talent and goodwill on the part of the faculty members: it is predominantly a problem of structural relations.

Schwab's diagnosis of the problems with regard to curriculum research should be read alongside Veblen's and Clifford and Guthrie's strictures about the structural and academic relationships between university faculties of education and schooling. For here we have a second example of 'goal displacement'. Veblen (1962: 15) said: 'The difference between the modern university and the lower schools is broad and simple; not so much a difference of degree as of kind.' This distinctiveness of purpose and mission

unavoidably leads them to court a specious appearance of scholarship, and so to invest their technological discipline with a degree of pedantry and sophistication, whereby it is hoped to give these schools and their work some scientific and scholarly prestige.

(Veblen 1962: 15)

The resonance of Veblen's strictures has been confirmed in Clifford and Guthrie's work:

Our thesis is that schools of education, particularly those located on the campuses of prestigious research universities, have become ensnared improvidently in the academic and political cultures of their institutions and have neglected their professional allegiances. They are like marginal men, aliens in their own worlds. They have seldom succeeded in satisfying the scholarly norms of their campus letters and science colleagues, and they are simultaneously estranged from their practising professional peers. The more forcefully they have rowed toward the shores of scholarly research, the more distant they have become from the public schools they are duty bound to serve. Conversely, systematic efforts at addressing the applied problems of public schools have placed schools of education at risk on their own campuses.

(Clifford and Guthrie 1988: 3–4)

In short, the schools of education may have entered into a devil's bargain when they entered the university milieu. The result was that their mission changed from being primarily concerned with matters central to the practice of schooling, towards issues of status passage through more conventional university scholarship. The resulting dominance of conventional 'disciplinary' modes has had disastrous impact on educational research.

It may not be true that, as Adam Smith said, 'every profession is a conspiracy against the people'. It is, however, certainly true that professional groups construct their 'missions' in terms of the pursuit of status and resources, as well as ideals. Hence, faculties of education have codified and created bodies of knowledge to maximize the terms of the devil's bargain. Bodies of knowledge were created with two major functions: first, the creation of a corpus of 'expert knowledge' with which to instruct trainee teachers; secondly, and closely allied to this, to maximize status and esteem within the university milieu. Disciplinary theory served both purposes and symbolically enshrines the essentially academic and scholarly purposes of the faculties of education. If a side effect of these strategies was to reduce field-based inquiry and collaboration, this, it seems, was once judged a price worth paying.

The devil's bargain on the part of education was an especially pernicious form of a more general displacement of discourse and debate which surrounded the evolution of university knowledge production. University knowledge evolved as separate and distinct from public knowledge for, as C. Wright Mills noted:

Men of knowledge do not orient themselves exclusively toward the total society, but to special segments of that society with special demands, criteria of validity, of significant knowledge, of pertinent problems, etc. It is through integration of these demands and expectations of particular audiences which can be effectively located in the social structure, that men of knowledge organize their own work, define their data, seize upon their problems.

(Mills 1979: 613)

In Mills's view, such a structural location of 'men of knowledge' (sic) in the university could have profound implications for public discourse and debate. Mills believed this would happen if the knowledge produced in this way did not have public relevance, particularly if it was not related to public and practical concerns:

> Only where publics and leaders are responsive and responsible are human affairs in democratic order, and only when knowledge has public relevance is this order possible. Only when mind has an autonomous basis, independent of power, but powerfully related to it, can it exert its force in the shaping of human affairs. Such a position is democratically possible only when there exists a free and knowledgeable public, to which men of knowledge may address themselves, and to which men of power are truly responsible. Such a public and such men – either of power or of knowledge, do not now prevail, and accordingly, knowledge does not now have democratic relevance in America.
>
> (Mills 1979: 613)

The dilemma facing producers of knowledge, which Mills describes, is acute when that knowledge relates to schooling. In the schools, knowledge is transmitted to future generations. If our knowledge of such knowledge transmission is flawed, we are doubly imperilled: schooling is so intimately related to the social order that if either our knowledge of schooling is inadequate or it has no public relevance, then major aspects of social and political life are obscured. In a real way, the future of democracy in any meaningful sense is called in to question.

Hence the question 'whither educational research?' is one of great importance. Mills, I think, comes close to the nature of our dilemma and spells out the implications of the devil's bargain when he talks of the way 'men of knowledge' orient themselves to 'special segments of society'. This has been the fate of much educational and curriculum theory and the effect has been that, as Mills put it, different groups 'talk past each other'. With few exceptions, I would argue this is precisely the relationship between faculties of education and school practitioners: they constitute a model of how to talk past each other.

The crucial point to grasp, however, is that the communication and ongoing displacement between theory and practice is not an intrinsic, but rather a socially structured problem. New structures of collaboration and forms of knowledge might help ease the current problems.

One way to summarize the dilemma is that the structural location of faculties of education have led to a particular politics of representation with regard to schools in general and teachers in particular. The politics of representation has much to do with being 'ensnared improvidently in the academic and political cultures of universities', and thereby ensnared in the dominant missions and status passages of those institutions. To achieve scholarly esteem through spurious objectivity and scientistic proceduralism, schooling and teachers have been represented by education scholars in particular ways. In the postwar period, teachers were represented most commonly in large-scale surveys or a variety of statistical calculations and correlations. Where more qualitative data was presented, the teacher was viewed as a somewhat timeless figure who conducted his [normally his] role in response to the traditional expectations of society. Diversity, ambivalence, marginality, let alone resistance and contestation, were seldom glimpsed in their accounts.

In the 1970s and 1980s, more qualitative methods opened up greater knowledge of school processes, procedures and practices, but even then I judged:

> Researchers had not confronted the complexity of the schoolteacher as an active agent making his or her own history. Researchers, even when they had stopped treating the teacher as numerical aggregate, historical footnote or unproblematic role incumbent still treated teachers as interchangeable types unchanged by circumstance or time.
>
> (Goodson 1992: 4)

The politics of representation associated with the devil's bargain have, therefore, had a pernicious effect in representing teachers. The task is to use the current crisis to reorder priorities, and develop patterns of research and representation which rescue silent lives and silenced voices. A new collaborative mode focusing on the teacher's life and work but retaining a reflective critical and theoretical dimension is required, and faculties of education must play a proactive part.

The problems of faculties of education are particularly worrisome because of the political climate in which we currently operate. I should make it clear that my mission, in tentatively seeking to reconceptualize educational research, is to revive and reconstitute one of the important missions so often neglected inside faculties of education; the critical and theoretical examination and elucidation of schooling, and of the institutionalized practices which are undertaken in schools.

What is urgently required is a relationship between faculties of education and school practitioners which is meaningful, vivid and vital. It is my view that, unless this relationship is rapidly explored and reinforced, new agendas will gather pace globally. In most Western countries, educational patterns are being challenged and reconstituted. A particularly salient feature is the move towards more 'practical matters'. Normally, this means a focus on classroom-based work and classroom-based training. In its extreme and mindless form, this focuses on funding the direct training of teachers in schools and promoting the marginalization of faculties of education, or the restructuring of their mission to exclusively practical matters.

Paul Hirst, an eloquent advocate of foundational disciplines, has argued that 'initial teacher education programmes are now subject to a set of criteria promulgated by the Secretary of State for Education and require considerable *practical* [my emphasis] preparation. There has, therefore, been an '*inevitable decrease in the attention to theoretical matters* [my emphasis] in these programmes' (Hirst 1989: 272). In summarizing these developments (and Hirst was writing before the culminating phase), he says:

> in-service teacher education is now concentrating severely on the *practical demands of new legislation* [my emphasis] . . . research has had little influence. Advanced study of a systematic kind is now much reduced.
>
> (Hirst 1989: 272)

The situation in Britain reflects in extreme form the current changes affecting a good deal of teacher education throughout the Western world. What is unusual about the British response is the hysterical tone of so much of the opposition to 'educational theorists' – normally referred to as 'trendy educational theorists' or 'theorists from the sixties'. The result of this hysteria has been to push the reforms which seek to embrace practical matters further than has been attempted in most other countries.

This hysteria apart, it is clear that North American, European and Australian states are following similar trajectories in pursuing a more utilitarian profile for teacher education. For this reason, let me briefly peruse the effects of changes in British teacher education in the postwar period.

The relationship which I want to explore most closely is the relationship between the research and study aspects of teacher education, and the pre-service and in-service training needs. Most commentators have agreed that in the period following the McNair Report of 1944, university schools of education held to a reasonably balanced mission with regard to theory and practical preparation. Some years ago, I reviewed the emergence of this balanced professional mission and its consolidation in the postwar years (Goodson 1993).

University schools of education were given responsibility through their area training organizations for the provision of pre-service training, not only in their own departments but also in many 'training colleges'.

> It was, however, the departments and schools of education that were to pioneer courses in the study of education as a significant contribution to the professional education of teachers. Courses were begun in educational psychology, in the history of education, in educational

measurement, in experimental educational research, child development and in the philosophy of education.

(Taylor 1987: 14)

From the first, then, university schools of education established 'foundational' disciplines as the basis of educational study. This foundational focus caused a bifurcation in the early educational research and teaching, as presented to the new cohorts of students:

> Much that these early students were taught was intellectually exciting and personally stimulating. But *it was redolent of its own reality, not that of the school and the classroom* [my emphasis].

(Taylor 1987: 14)

Philip Taylor adds: 'Even when sociology of education, curriculum studies and educational administration came to be added to the range of courses, this remained true, though less so' (Taylor 1987: 14).

The courses of study taught in schools of education moved from a part-time to a largely full-time basis. Postgraduate training of teachers with degrees took place in year-long courses at the university. Teachers often spent a year on secondment to the university to complete a Masters course.

> The standard of work achieved by the students was sound if academic. Classroom teachers were taught how to reflect on their teaching, on pupil learning, on the structure and organization of schools, to question educational assumptions and to understand how sexism and racism operated in the classroom.

(Taylor 1987: 14)

These courses then enshrined the 'theoretical mission' of university study as well as practical preparation. But the theoretical mission should not be divorced from the assumption of practical effect. At its best, theory works back into informed and improved practice. Hence,

> Some students used their new knowledge to render worthwhile changes in their teaching, to influence colleagues, to introduce new ways of examining, to improve the quality of discourse at staff meetings and the management and efficiency of teaching departments.

(Taylor 1987: 14)

The presence of a diverse and informed student clientele provides enormous ongoing support to the work of educational scholarship in the university schools of education. At its best, in the university, the work could move between theoretical preoccupation and practical predilection in ways that challenged both.

But too often, it is true, this arbitration between theory and practice was replaced by a colonizing university discourse of theory. This kind of theory 'redolent of its own reality' became the monolithic enemy of those seeking to reform teacher education among the New Right followers of Thatcher's Conservative Party victory in 1979. A problem of balance, of how to reinstate and reinscribe a balance between theory and practice in the university faculties of education, was reinterpreted as a sole and simple problem of location. As a result (like the Narodniks in nineteenth-century Russia with their revolutionary 'back to the land' movement), we saw a 'back to the schools' movement develop. During the 1980s, this practical fundamentalist programme made steady progress.

The initial period was one of incidental attrition. In the mid-1980s, money began to be redirected away from faculties of education. Social science research studentships rapidly decreased in number: so therefore did full-time Masters and Doctoral students. More significantly, in April 1987, the 'pool' of money – by which local education authorities paid for the secondment of serving teachers – was drained. Slowly the 'critical mass' of students required to keep up Masters and research degrees disappeared. Deprived of this student clientele and associated research discourse, a good deal of faculty research also dried up, particularly as faculty now became more and more concerned with designing short school-based courses which were 'practical and relevant'.

Attrition changed to outright redirection with Kenneth Clarke's new policy announced at the North of England Conference in January 1992. Clarke announced that, at least in all secondary school subjects, henceforth 80 per cent of training would be moved from the university faculty of education schools to the secondary school. Although this was subsequently changed, the theoretical importance of the announcement was substantial, especially the implicit demeaning of university theorists and their courses.

This demeaning of university educationalists was clear in the styling of schools as having a 'leading responsibility' in teacher education.

> Schools will have a leading responsibility for training students to teach their specialist subject, to assess pupils and to manage classes; and for supervising students and assessing their competence in these respects.
>
> (DES 1992: para. 14)

Universities were moved back into a more distant 'hands off' role of academic validation and accreditation. These priorities were reiterated in subsequent government pronouncements. In 1998, the Teacher Training Agency pronounced:

> Those training to be teachers undertake substantial periods of school-based training and school teachers play a substantial part in planning and teaching the courses.
>
> (TTA 1998: 2)

In Britain, I suspect the ongoing over-embrace of the practical will lead to a collapse of the academic and theoretical mission of faculties of education. Logically, this would seem to lead to questions being raised as to why such faculties, without substantial academic and theoretical missions, should any longer be located within the universities. Such questions may arise forcibly as universities seek to restructure themselves because of financial retrenchment (see Cochran-Smith and Fries 2001).

In a more general global sense, the 'problem of balance', which arose when faculties of education joined universities, may lead to a radical change. Because of the sharp pendulum swing away from too much theory 'redolent of its own reality' to a version of 'practical relevance', the whole basis of the enterprise could be at risk. In short, in this time of change, we need to strike a new balance between theory, critique and practical matters. If we cannot strike such a balance, I believe the main mission and the overarching rationale for university faculties of education will begin to collapse.

From the teacher's viewpoint, such a collapse may not seem like a cause for concern. The ivory towers have built walls and become distant. However, the resources and expertise and, indeed, status of faculties of education do play a role in representing teachers and could – and now *must* – play a vastly extended role. As a profession represented by university faculties involved in training teachers, teaching gains from the status 'pecking order' of Western institutional life. Even if too symbolic, even if only symbolic, this is an important rationale for continued university involvement.

The university provides a major legitimating base for professional status. Without the faculties, a whole resource base would be lost to new generations of teachers: at their least, the faculties represent time and space for reflective work. There are quiet rooms, resource centres and libraries, together with the critical and intellectual resources of the faculty. But these resources must be more usefully employed in a rejuvenated and reconceptualized collaborative pact between the university faculties and the school practitioners. The new collaborative mode must be reciprocal, equal and respectful, but it must never lose the reflective and intellectual edge which the best educational practices and study demand.

Developing collaboration and reinscribing a theoretical mission

The concluding issue is how to develop collaborative modes in ways which maintain, revive and reinscribe theoretical and critical missions within teacher education. In current political times, this is clearly not an easy act to accomplish, even when thinking theoretically, but it does mean that we need to look closely at the potential collaboration between teachers and externally located researchers in faculties of education. While I believe that the best mechanism for improving practice is if teachers in an ongoing way research and reflect upon their practice, I do not believe that a narrow focus on practice in collaborating on research, a panacea that is politically popular at the moment, will take us very far. There are many reasons for this contention. Let me focus on two. First, education is far more than a practical matter. Practice constitutes a good deal more than the technical things teachers do in classrooms. Education is a personal matter as well as a political matter. The way teachers interact in the classroom relates in a considerable manner to who they are and to their whole approach to life. It would be important, therefore, to have a collaborative form of research which links and analyses the teacher's life and work.

Secondly, the interactive practices of classes are subject to constant change, particularly at the moment political and constitutional change. These often take the form of new government guidelines. These 'preactive' political actions set crucial parameters for interactive classroom practice. Preactive action thereby constrains and facilitates interactive possibilities. In their collaborative study, teachers and externally located researchers need, therefore, to focus both on the preactive and the interactive. To stay only with practice as a politically and socially constructed form is inevitably to involve teachers in the implementation and acceptance of initiatives which are generated elsewhere. This would make collaboration and research into a form of political quietism as the focus of the collaboration would be the form of practice that has *already* been politically determined and constructed.

For these reasons, I would be against the notion that our focus for collaborative work between teachers and externally located researchers should be mainly upon practice. In some ways, regrettably, this is the logical outcome of the phrase 'teacher as researcher' (a movement whose value position I strongly support), for the converse is the 'researcher as teacher'. As we have noted, the teacher's work is profoundly politically and socially constructed. The parameters to practice, whether they be political or biographical, range over an extremely wide terrain. To narrow our focus to 'practice as defined' is to ensure that our collaborative work may fall victim to historical circumstances and political tendencies. At the moment, governments in many Western countries are seeking to transform the teacher's practice into that of a technician; a deliverer of predesigned packages, guidelines and assessments. To accept these definitions, and to focus our collaboration and research on practice so defined, is to accept these visions and objectives.

While, of course, some of the more valuable, theoretical and collaborative work within these traditions has sought to extend and transcend the politically dominant definitions of practice, this does not avoid the substance of the critique. For, by starting our research and collaboration, by focusing on practice in this way, the initiative for defining our very starting point has been conceded to politicians and bureaucrats. It is my profound belief that to sponsor more autonomous and collaborative work we need to adopt a wider lens of inquiry. This lens of inquiry could take a number of forms. It could focus on critical incidents in teaching, as David Tripp (1994) has eloquently argued; it could focus on theories of context (Goodson 1994b; Goodson and Sikes 2001); it could focus on the teacher's life and work; it could focus on teachers' stories or narratives (see Clandinin and Connelly 1998). It should, in short, be possible to develop a broader lens for our collaborative educational study in the future. Much of the emerging work in the areas I have listed now indicates that a rich flow of dialogue and data can be assembled through broadening our lens of inquiry and collaboration. Moreover, this broadened focus may (and I stress *may*) allow teachers greater authority and control in collaborative research than has often appeared to be the case with practice-oriented study. The focus in that work has been on the teacher's practice, almost the teacher *as* practice. What is now required is a collaborative modality that listens, above all, to the person at whom 'development' and 'implementation' is aimed. This means strategies should now be explored and developed which facilitate and maximize the potential for the teacher's involvement in collaborative work. I believe this strategy for developing collaboration and reinscribing the theoretical mission is well underway, and it behoves us to push much harder to ensure that this kind of work sets up an articulate counterculture to the current initiatives that occupy 'the high ground' in so many Western countries.

In the next chapters, I therefore review some of the work on teachers' lives and teachers' stories that has been emerging over the past two decades. By focusing on this work and identifying some of the major possibilities and pitfalls, I hope to set the scene for links in this work to our understandings of educational change and improvement.

three

Representing teachers: bringing teachers back in

The representational crisis

As we saw in Chapter 2, educational study is undergoing one of those recurrent swings of the pendulum for which the field is noted. But, as the contemporary world and global economies are transformed by rapid and accelerating change, such pendulum swings in scholarly paradigms seem to be alarmingly exacerbated. Also in this chapter, we saw how the practical fundamentalists were arguing for a return to practice and an evacuation of educational theory. Practical fundamentalism and increased central control turn out to be remarkably compatible – an arranged marriage; the theorist has been replaced by the politician in patterns of educational policy and expertise (Cochran-Smith and Fries 2001).

In this chapter, we renew some of the responses to practical fundamentalism and critiques of disciplinary theory. In particular, we look at the increasing advocacy of teacher narratives and teacher stories as a form of research that gets us closer to teachers' practice, to their personal practical knowledge. This moves us from educational research as disciplinary study and disciplinary grand narrative to a different mode of representation.

Hence, at the beginning of the book, we see a set of responses to a specific structural dilemma in which educational study has become enmeshed. But alongside this, the field is becoming engulfed (though more slowly than in many fields) by a crisis of scholarly representation. A specific structural dilemma now becomes allied with a wider representational crisis. Jameson (1984: viii) has summarized the latter crisis succinctly, as arising from the growing challenge to 'an essentially realistic epistemology, which conceives of representation as the production, for subjectivity, of an objectivity that lies outside it'. Jameson wrote this in the foreword to Lyotard's *The Postmodern Condition*. For Lyotard, the old modes of representation no longer work. He calls for an incredulity towards these old canonical metanarratives and says, 'the grand narrative has lost its credibility, regardless of what mode of unification is used, regardless of whether it is a speculative narrative or a narrative of emancipation' (Lyotard 1984: 37).

Returning to the field of educational study, we see that in response to the distant, divorced and disengaged nature of aspects of educational study in universities, some scholars have responded by embracing the 'practical', by celebrating the teacher as practitioner.

My intention here is to explore in detail one of these movements aiming to focus on teachers' knowledge – particularly the genre which focuses on teachers' stories and narratives. This movement has arisen from the crises of structural displacement and of representation briefly outlined. Hence the reasons for this new genre are understandable, the motivations creditable. As we see, the representational crisis arises from the central dilemma of trying to capture the lived experience of scholars and of teachers within a text. The experience of other lives is, therefore, rendered textual by an author. At root, this is a perilously difficult act and Denzin has cogently inveighed against the very aspiration:

> If the text becomes the agency that records and represents the voices of the other, then the other becomes a person who is spoken for. They do not talk, the text talks for them. It is the agency that interprets their words, thoughts, intentions, and meanings. So a doubling of agency occurs, for behind the text as agent-for-the-other, is the author of the text doing the interpreting.
>
> (Denzin 1993: 17)

Denzin, then, is arguing that we have a classic case of academic colonization, or even cannibalization: 'The other becomes an extension of the author's voice. The authority of their "original" voice is now subsumed within the larger text and its double-agency' (1993: 17).

Given the scale of this representational crisis, one can quickly see how the sympathetic academic might wish to reduce interpretation, even collaboration, and return to the role of 'scribe'. At least in such passivity sits the aspiration to reduce colonization. In this moment of representational crisis, the doors open to the educational scholar as facilitator, as conduit for the teacher, to tell her/his story or narrative. The genuine voice of the oppressed subject uncontaminated by active human collaboration; teachers talking about their practice, providing us with personal and practical insights into their expertise.

Here, maybe, is a sanctuary, an inner sanctum, beyond the representational crisis, beyond academic colonization. The nirvana of the narrative, the Valhalla of voice; it is an understandable and appealing project.

The narrative turn/The turn to narrative

So the turn to teachers' narratives and stories is, at one level, a thoroughly understandable response to the way in which teachers have tended to be represented in so much educational study. The teacher has been represented to serve our scholarly purposes.

Given this history and the goal displacement of educational study noted, it is therefore laudable that new narrative movements are concentrating on the teachers' presentation of themselves. This is a welcome antidote to so much misrepresentation and representation in past scholarship, and it opens up avenues of fruitful investigation and debate. The narrative movement provides then a catalyst for pursuing understandings of the teacher's life and work. In many ways, the movement reminds me of the point raised by Molly Andrews in her elegant study of elderly political activists. She summarizes the posture of those psychologists who have studied such activists:

> When political psychology has taken to analysing the behaviour of political activists it has tended to do so from a thoroughly external perspective. That is to say, that rarely have their thought processes been described, much less analysed, from their own point of view. Yet it is at least possible that a very good way to learn about the psychology of political activists is to listen to what they have to say about their own lives.
>
> (Andrews 1991: 20)

What Andrews says can be seen as analogous to a good deal of our scholarly representation of teachers where they are seen as interchangeable and essentially depersonalized. In 1981, I argued that many accounts presented teachers as timeless and interchangeable role incumbents, but that

> The pursuit of personal and biographical data might rapidly challenge the assumption of interchangeability. Likewise, by tracing the teachers' life as it evolved over time – throughout the teachers' career and through several generations – the assumption of timelessness might also be remedied. *In understanding something so intensely personal as teaching it is critical we know about the person the teacher is.* Our paucity of knowledge in this area is a manifest indictment of the range of our sociological imagination.
>
> (Goodson 1981: 69)

The argument for listening to teachers is, therefore, a substantial and long overdue one. Narratives, stories, journals, action research and phenomenology have all contributed to a growing movement to provide opportunities for teacher representations. In the case of stories and narratives, Kathy Carter has provided a valuable summary of this growing movement in the early years of its educational incarnation:

> With increasing frequency over the past several years we, as members of a community of investigator–practitioners, have been telling stories about teaching and teacher education rather than simply reporting correlation coefficients or generating lists of findings. This trend has been upsetting to some who mourn the loss of quantitative precision and, they would argue, scientific rigour. For many of us, however, these stories capture, more than scores or mathematical formulae ever can, the richness and indeterminacy of our experiences as teachers and the complexity of our understandings of what teaching is and how others can be prepared to engage in this profession.
>
> It is not altogether surprising, then, that this attraction to stories has evolved into an explicit attempt to use the literatures on 'story' or 'narrative' to define both the method and the object of inquiry in teaching and teacher education. Story has become, in other words, more than simply a rhetorical device for expressing sentiments about teachers or candidates for the teaching profession. It is now, rather, a central focus for conducting research in the field.
>
> (Carter 1993: 5)

Story and history

The emphasis upon teachers' stories and narratives encouragingly signifies a new turn in presenting teachers. It is a turn that deserves to be taken very seriously, for we have to be sure that we are turning in the right direction. Like all new genres, stories and narratives are Janus-faced; they may move us forward into new insights or backwards into constrained consciousness – and sometimes simultaneously.

This uncertainty is well stated in Carter's summary of 'The place of story in the study of teaching and teacher education':

> Anyone with even a passing familiarity with the literatures on story soon realizes, however, that these are quite turbulent intellectual waters and quickly abandons the expectation of safe passage toward the resolution, once and for all, of the many puzzles and dilemmas we face in advancing our knowledge of teaching. Much needs to be learned about the nature of story and its value to our common enterprise, and about the wide range of purposes, approaches, and claims made by those who have adopted story as a central analytical

framework. What does story capture and what does it leave out? How does this notion fit within the emerging sense of the nature of teaching and what it means to educate teachers? These and many other critical questions need to be faced if story is to become more than a loose metaphor for everything from a paradigm or world view to a technique for bringing home a point in a lecture on a Thursday afternoon.

(Carter 1993: 5)

But what is the nature of the turbulence in the intellectual waters surrounding stories, and will they serve to drown the new genre? The turbulence is multifaceted, but here I want to focus on the relationship between stories and the social context in which they are embedded. For stories exist in history – they are, in fact, deeply located in time and space. Stories work differently in different social contexts and historical times – they can be put to work in different ways.

Stories then should not only be *narrated* but also *located*. This argues that we should move beyond the self-referential individual narration to a wider contextualized, collaborative mode. Again, Carter hints at both the enormous appeal and the underlying worry about narrative and story. At the moment, the appeal is substantial after long years of silencing, but the dangers are more shadowy. I believe that unless those dangers are confronted now, narrative and story may end up silencing, or at least marginalizing in new ways, the very people to whom it appears to give voice.

For many of us, these arguments about the personal, storied nature of teaching and about voice, gender, and power in our professional lives ring very true. We can readily point to instances in which we have felt excluded by researchers' language or powerless in the face of administrative decrees and evaluation instruments presumably bolstered by scientific evidence. And we have experienced the indignities of gender bias and presumptions. We feel these issues deeply, and opening them to public scrutiny, especially through the literature in our field, is a cause for celebration. At the same time, we must recognize that this line of argument creates a very serious crisis for our community. One can easily imagine that the analysis summarized here, if pushed ever so slightly forward, leads directly to a rejection of all generalizations about teaching as distortions of teachers' real stories and as complicity with the power elite, who would make teachers subservient. From this perspective, only the teacher owns her or his story and its meaning. As researchers and teacher educators, we can only serve by getting this message across to the larger society and, perhaps, by helping teachers to come to know their own stories. Seen in this light, much of the activity in which we engage as scholars in teaching becomes illegitimate if not actually harmful.

(Carter 1993: 8)

Carolyn Steedman, in her marvellous work, *Landscape for a Good Woman*, speaks of this danger. She says, 'Once a story is told, it ceases to story: it becomes a piece of history, an interpretative device' (Steedman 1986: 143). In this sense, a story 'works' when its rationale is comprehended and its historical significance grasped. As Bristow (1991: 117) has argued, 'The more skilled we become at understanding the history involved in these very broadly defined stories, the more able will we be to identify the ideological function of narratives – how they designate a place for us within their structure of telling.' In reviewing Steedman's work and its power to understand patriarchy and the dignity of women's lives, Bristow talks about her unswerving attention to

> the ways in which life writing can bring its writers to the point of understanding how their lives have already been narrated – according to a prefigurative script, Steedman never loses sight of how writers may develop skills to rewrite the life script in which they find themselves.
>
> (Bristow 1991: 114)

This, I think, focuses acutely on the dangers of a belief that merely by allowing people to 'narrate', we in any serious way give them voice *and* agency. The narration of a prefigurative script is a celebration of an existing power relation. More often, and this is profoundly true for teachers, the question is how to 'rewrite the life script'. Narration, then, can work in many ways, but clearly it can work to give voice to a celebration of scripts of domination. Narration can both reinforce domination or rewrite domination. Stories and narratives are not an unquestioned good: it all depends. And above all, it depends on how they relate to history and to social context.

Again, Andrews's work on the lives of political activists captures the limitation of so much of the developmental psychologists' study of lives, and it is analogous to so much work on teacher narratives:

> In Western capitalist democracies, where most of the work on development originates, many researchers tend to ignore the importance of the society–individual dialectic, choosing to focus instead on more particularized elements, be they personality idiosyncrasies, parental relationships, or cognitive structures, as if such aspects of the individual's make-up could be neatly compartmentalized, existing in a contextual vacuum.
>
> (Andrews 1991: 13)

The version of 'personal' that has been constructed and worked for in some Western countries is a particular version, an individualistic version, of being a person. It is unrecognizable to much of the rest of the world. But so many of the stories and narratives we have of teachers work unproblematically and without comment with this version of personal being and personal knowledge. Masking the limits of individualism, such accounts often present 'isolation, estrangement, and loneliness . . . as autonomy, independence and self-reliance' (Andrews 1991: 13).

Andrews concludes that if we ignore social context, we deprive ourselves and our collaborators of meaning and understanding. She says:

> it would seem apparent that the context in which human lives are lived is central to the core of meaning in those lives. Researchers should not, therefore, feel at liberty to discuss or analyse how individuals perceive meaning in their lives and in the world around them, while ignoring the content and context of that meaning.
>
> (Andrews 1991: 13)

This, I believe, has been all too common a response among these educational researchers working with teachers' stories and narratives. Content has been embraced and celebrated, context has not been sufficiently developed. Cynthia Chambers has summarized this posture and its dangers in reviewing work on teachers' narratives:

> These authors offer us the naive hope that if teachers learn 'to tell and understand their *own* story' they will be returned to their rightful place at the centre of curriculum planning and reform. And yet, their method leaves each teacher a 'blackbird singing in the dead of night'; isolated, and sadly ignorant of how his/her song is part of a much larger singing of the world. If everyone is singing their own song, who is listening? How can we hear the larger conversation of humankind in which our own history teacher is embedded and perhaps concealed?
>
> (Chambers 1991: 354)

Likewise, Salina Shrofel, in reviewing the same book, highlights the dangers:

> Focus on the personal and on practice does not appear to lead practitioners or researchers/writers to analyse practice as theory, as social structure, or as a manifestation of political and economic systems. This limitation of vision implicit in the narrative approach serves as a constraint on curriculum reform. Teachers will, as did the teachers cited by Connelly and Clandinin, make changes in their own classroom curricula but will not perform the questioning and challenging of theory, structure, and ideology that will lead to radical and extensive curriculum reform.
>
> It can be argued that the challenge of running a classroom fully occupies the teachers and that questions of theory, structure, and ideology don't affect the everyday lives (practical knowledge) of teachers and are relegated to 'experts'. However, there are many dangers in separating

practice from these other questions. First, as Connelly and Clandinin point out, it ignores the dynamic relationship of theory and practice. Second, it ignores the fact that schools are intricately and inextricably part of the social fabric and of the political and economic system which dominates. Third, because curriculum reform is implemented in the classroom by teachers, separating teachers from these other aspects might negatively affect radical and widespread curriculum reform. To avoid these dangers, either the narrative method will have to be extended, or it will need to be supplemented with a process that encourages teachers to look beyond the personal.

(Shrofel 1991: 64–5)

In summary, should stories and narratives be a way of giving voice to a particular way of being, or should the genre serve as an introduction to alternative ways of being? Consciousness is constructed rather than autonomously produced; hence, giving voice to consciousness may give voice to the constructor at least as much as the speaker. If social context is left out this will likely happen.

The truth is that many times a life storyteller will neglect the structural context of their lives, or interpret such contextual forces from a biased point of view. As Denzin (1989: 74) says, 'Many times a person will act as if he or she made his or her own history when, in fact, he or she was forced to make the history he or she lived.' He gives an example from his 1986 study of alcoholics: 'You know I made the last four months by myself. I haven't used or drank. I'm really proud of myself. I did it' (Denzin 1989: 74–5). A friend, listening to this account commented:

You know you were under a court order all last year. You didn't do this on your own. You were forced to, whether you want to accept this fact or not. You also went to AA and NA. Listen Buster, you did what you did because you had help and because you were afraid and thought you had no other choice. Don't give me this, 'I did it on my own' crap.

(1989: 74–5)

The speaker replies, 'I know. I just don't like to admit it.' Denzin concludes:

This listener invokes two structural forces, the state and AA, which accounted in part for this speaker's experience. To have secured only the speaker's account, without a knowledge of his biography and personal history, would have produced a biased interpretation of his situation.

(1989: 74–5)

The great virtue of stories is that they particularize and make concrete our experiences. This, however, should be the *starting point* in our social and educational study. Stories can so richly move us into the terrain of the social, into insights into the socially constructed nature of our experiences. Feminist sociology has often treated stories in this way. As Hilary Graham says, 'Stories are pre-eminently ways of relating individuals and events to social contexts, ways of weaving personal experiences into their social fabric' (see Armstrong 1987: 14). Again, Carolyn Steedman speaks of this two-step process. First the story particularizes, details and historicizes – then at second stage, the 'urgent need' to develop theories of context:

> The fixed townscapes of Northampton and Leeds that Hoggart and Seabrook have described show endless streets of houses, where mothers who don't go out to work order the domestic day, where men are masters, and children, when they grow older, express gratitude for the harsh discipline meted out to them. The first task is to particularize this profoundly a-historical landscape (and so this book details a mother who was a working woman and a single parent, and a father who wasn't a patriarch). And once the landscape is detailed and historicized in this way, the urgent need becomes to find a way of theorizing the result of such difference and particularity, not in order to find a description that can be universally applied (the point is *not* to say that all working-class childhoods are the same, nor that experience of them produces unique psychic structures) but so that the people in exile, the inhabitants of the long streets, may start to use the auto-biographical 'I', and tell the stories of their life.
>
> (Steedman 1986: 16)

The story, then, provides a starting point for developing further understandings of the social construction of subjectivity. If the teachers' stories stay at the level of the personal and practical, we forego that opportunity. Speaking of the narrative method focusing on personal and practical teachers' knowledge, Willinsky writes:

> I am concerned that a research process intended to recover the personal and experiential (aspects or not?) would pave over this construction site in its search for an overarching unity in the individual's narrative.
>
> (Willinsky 1989: 259)

Personal and practical teachers' stories may, therefore, act not to further our understandings, but merely to celebrate the particular constructions of the 'teacher' which have been wrought by political and social contestation. Teachers' stories can be stories of particular political victories and political settlements. Because of their limitation of focus, teachers' stories – as stories of the personal and practical – are likely to be limited in this manner.

A story of action within a story of context

This section comes from a phrase often used by Lawrence Stenhouse (1975), who was concerned in much of his work to introduce a historical dimension to our studies of schooling and curriculum. While himself a leading advocate of the teacher as researcher and pioneer of that method, he was worried about the proliferation of practical stories of action, individualized and isolated, unique and idiosyncratic, as our stories of action and our lives are. But as we have seen, lives and stories link with broader social scripts – they are not just individual productions, they are also social constructions. We must make sure that individual and practical stories do not reduce, seduce and reproduce particular teacher mentalities, and lead us away from broader patterns of understanding.

Let us try to situate the narrative moment in the historical moment – for the narrative movement itself could be located in a theory of context. In some ways the movement has analogies with the existential movement of the 1940s. Existentialists believed that only through our actions could we define ourselves. Our role, existentialists judged, was to invent ourselves as individuals, then, as in Sartre's (1961) trilogy *Les Chemins de la Liberté*, we would be 'free', especially from the claims of society and the 'others'.

Existentialism existed at a particular historical moment following the massive trauma of the Second World War, and in France, where it developed most strongly, of the protracted German occupation. George Melly judges that existentialism grew out of this historial context.

> My retrospective explanation is that it provided a way of exorcising the collective guilt of the occupation, to reduce the betrayals, the collaboration, the blind eye, the unjustified compromise, to an acceptable level. We know now that the official post-war picture of France under the Nazis was a deliberate whitewash and that almost everyone knew it, and suppressed the knowledge. Existentialism, by insisting on the complete isolation of the individual as free to act, but free to do nothing else, as culpable or heroic but *only* within those limits, helped absolve the notion of corporate and national ignominy.
>
> (Melly 1993: 9)

Above all, then, an individualizing existentialism freed people from the battle of ideologies, freed them from the awfulness of political and military conflict. Individualized existentialism provided a breathing space away from power and politics.

But the end of the Second World War did not provide an end to politics, only a move from hot war to cold war. As we know, ideologies continued their contest in the most potentially deadly manner. During this period, narratives of personal life began to blossom. Brightman (see Sage 1994) has developed a fascinating picture of how Mary McCarthy's personal narratives grew out of the witch-hunting period of Joe McCarthy. Her narratives moved us from the 'contagion of ideas' to the personal 'material world'. Mary McCarthy could 'strip ideas of their abstract character and return them to the social world from whence they came' (quoted in Sage 1994: 5). In Irving Howes's memorable phrase, as 'ideology crumbled, personality bloomed' (Sage 1994: 5).

And so with the end of ideology, the end of the cold war, we see the proliferant blooming of personality, not least in the movement towards personal narratives and stories. Once again, the personal narrative, the practical story, celebrates the end of the trauma of the cold war and the need for a human space away from politics, away from power. It is a thoroughly understandable nirvana, but it assumes that power and politics have somehow ended. It assumes, in that wishful phrase, 'the end of history'.

In educational bureaucracies, power continues to be hierarchically administered. I have often asked administrators and educational bureaucrats why they support personal and practical forms of knowledge for teachers in the form of narratives and stories. Their comments often echo those of the 'true believers' in narrative method. But I always go on, after suitable pause and diversion to ask: 'What do you do on your leadership courses?' There, it is always 'politics as usual' management skills, quality assurance, micropolitical strategies, personnel training. Personal and practical stories for some, cognitive maps of power for others. So while the use of stories and narratives can provide a useful breathing space away from power, it does not suspend the continuing administration of power; indeed, it could well make this so much easier. Especially as, over time, teachers' knowledge would become more and more personal and practical – different 'mentalities'. Wholly different understandings of power would emerge, as between, say, teachers and school managers, teachers and administrators, teachers and some educational scholars.

Teachers' individual and practical stories certainly provide a breathing space. However, at one and the same time, they reduce the oxygen of broader understandings. The breathing space comes to look awfully like a vacuum, where history and social construction are somehow suspended.

In this way, teachers become divorced from what might be called the 'vernacular of power', the ways of talking and knowing which then become the prerogative of managers, administrators and academics. In this discourse, politics and micro-politics are the essence and currency of the interchange. Alongside this and in a sense facilitating this, a new 'vernacular of the particular, the personal and the practical' arises, which is specific to teachers.

This form of apartheid could easily emerge if teachers' stories and narratives remain singular and specific, personal and practical, particular and apolitical. Hence, it is a matter of some urgency that we develop stories of action within theories of context – contextualizing stories, if you like – which act against the kinds of divorce of the discourses that are all too readily imaginable.

Carter had begun to worry about just such a problem in her work on 'The place of story in the study of teaching and teacher education':

> And for those of us telling stories in our work, we will not serve the community well if we sanctify story-telling work and build an epistemology on it to the point that we simply substitute one paradigmatic domination for another *without challenging domination itself*. We must, then, become much more self conscious than we have been in the past about the issues involved in narrative and story, such as interpretation, authenticity, normative value, and what our purposes are for telling stories in the first place.
>
> (Carter 1993: 11)

Some of these worries about stories can be explored in scrutinizing the way in which powerful interest groups in society actually promote and employ storied material. In the next chapter, we turn to examples of the use of stories in the media as a way of exploring this complex but crucial issue.

four

The story so far: personal knowledge and the political

In this chapter, I continue my exploration of some forms of inquiry that are becoming influential within teacher education: forms of inquiry variously called 'stories', 'narratives', 'personal knowledge', 'practical knowledge', or, in one particular genre, 'personal practical knowledge' (see Clandinin and Connelly 1998).

As I noted in the earlier sections, I find myself highly sympathetic to the urge to generate new ways of producing, collaborating, representing and knowing. They offer a serious opportunity to question many of the implicit racial, class, or gender biases which existing modes of inquiry mystify while reproducing (see Giroux 1991). Storying and narratology are genres which allow us to move beyond (or to the side of) the main paradigms of inquiry – with their numbers, variables, psychometrics, psychologisms and decontextualized theories. The new genres have the potential for advancing educational research in representing the lived experience of schooling (Goodson and Hargreaves 1996; Goodson and Sikes 2001).

Because of this substantial potential, the new genres require very close scrutiny. For while they have some obvious strengths, there are, I think, some weaknesses which may prove incapacitating. If so, we may be sponsoring genres of inquiry in the name of empowerment, while, at the same time, effectively disempowering the very people and causes we seek to work with.

Personal knowledge and the cultural logic of postmodernity

Before embracing personal knowledge in the form of narratives and story, it is important to locate this genre within the emergent cultural patterns of contemporary societies and economies. While the pace of change at the moment is rapid, a good deal of evidence points to an increasingly aggrandizing centre or state acting to sponsor 'voices' at the level of interest groups, localities and peripheries. From the perspective of these groups, this may look like empowerment for oppressed aboriginals, the physically and mentally challenged, gays and lesbians, and other deserving groups. This is all long overdue. But we need to be aware of the overall social matrix. Specific empowerment can go hand-in-hand with overall social control.

Alongside these new voices, a systematic attack on median or secondary associations is underway on schools, universities, libraries, welfare agencies, and the like – an attack on many of the existing agencies of cultural mediation and production. Economic restructuring is being closely allied to cultural redefinition and there is a reduction of contextual and theoretical discourses, and an overall sponsorship of personal and practical forms of discourse and cultural production. The overall effect will be substantially to redraw existing modes of political and cultural analysis. In its place, we may end up with what Harvey (1989) calls the *tyranny of the local*, alongside what we might call the specificity of the personal. General patterns, social contexts and critical theories will be replaced by local stories and personal anecdotes (on *restructuring*, see Robertson 1997).

Denzin has commented on this in his critique of the rehabilitated 'life story movement':

> The cultural logics of late capitalism valorise the life story, autobiographical document because they keep the myth of the autonomous, free individual alive. This logic finds its modern roots on Rousseau's *Confessions*, a text perfectly fitted to the cultural logics of the new capitalist societies where a division between public and private had to be maintained, and where the belief in a pure, natural self was cherished. The logic of the confession reifies the concept of the self and turns it into a cultural commodity. The rise to power of the social sciences in the twentieth century corresponded to the rise of the modern surveillance state. That state required information on its citizens. Social scientists, of both qualitative and quantitative commitments, gathered information for this society. The recent return to the life story celebrates the importance of the individual under the conservative politics of late postmodernism.
>
> (Denzin 1992: 8–9)

Hence, in the cultural logic of late capital, the life story represents a form of cultural apparatus to accompany a newly aggrandizing state and market system. In the situation that is being 'worked for', the subject/state, consumer/market confrontation will be immediate. The range of secondary associations and bureaucracies which currently 'buffer' or mediate this pattern of social relations will be progressively reduced. The cultural buffer of theory, critique and political commentary will likewise wither. It will not be the state that withers (as in Marxist theory), but the critical theories and cultural critiques that stand against the state. In the 'end of history', we shall indeed see the closure of cultural contestation as evidenced in theoretical and critical discourse. In its place will stand a learned discourse comprising stories and practices, specific, local and located but divorced from understandings of social context and social process. In the next section, I review how this cultural redefinition is emerging in some aspects of the media.

The media context of personal knowledge

This section briefly examines the promotion of more personal stories at the level of the media. The promotional strategies at these levels pose questions, in whose interests the move to more personal knowledge is being undertaken. There is, after all, an 'opportunity cost' to the time being spent on personal stories – in a finite world of time, less time is thereby spent on other aspects, most notably on more wide-ranging political and social analysis.

The move towards storytelling is becoming pronounced in the media. This can be seen most clearly in the media of those countries which have retained, until recently, a strong tradition of political and cultural analysis. Michael Ignatieff, a Canadian working in Britain and one of the most elegant of cultural analysts, writes in the *Observer*: 'Whatever we hacks may piously profess, the media is not in the information business. It is in the storytelling business' (Ignatieff 1992: 21). He then details a range of new developments in the British media which evidence this trend. Storytelling and personal anecdotes are the powerful new fashion, he writes:

> As if to make this plain, ITN's *News at Ten* is reintroducing its 'And finally' end piece, 'traditionally devoted to animals, children and royalty'. After footage from Sarajevo, we'll be treated, for example, to the sight of some lovable ducks on a surfboard. The ducks are there not just to cheer us up but to reach those subliminal zones of ourselves which long to believe that the horror of Sarajevo is just so much nasty make-believe.
>
> The audience's longing for stories about ducks on surfboards is only one of the trends which is taking the media away from even notional attention to the real world. The other is the media's growing fascination with itself. The last few weeks have seen this obsession inflate to baroque extremes of narcissism. When Trevor McDonald gets the *News at Ten* job and Julia Somerville does not; when Sir David English vacates

one editor's chair and Simon Jenkins vacates another; when Andrew Neil snarls at the 'saintly' Andreas Whittam-Smith and the saint snarls back, I ask myself: does anybody care but us hacks?

(1992: 21)

Ignatieff notes that 'there's a price to pay when the media systematically concentrates on itself and ignores the world outside' (1992: 21). The opportunity cost of storytelling is that personal minutiae and anecdote replace cultural analysis. Above all, the 'story' is the other side of a closure on broad analysis, a failure of imagination. He writes:

> In this failure and in the media's amazing self-absorption, I see a shrinking in journalism's social imagination. What I know about the 1980s I owe to a journalism which believed that the challenge was to report Britain as if it was an unknown country: Bea Campbell's *Road to Wigan Pier*, for example, or Ian Jack's *Before the Oil Ran Out*. In place of genuine social curiosity, we have the killer interview, the media profile, the latest stale gossip. It's so fashionable we can't even see what a capitulation it represents.

(1992: 21)

The reasons for the promotion of the anecdote and personal story are both broadly cultural and political, but also specifically economic. They relate to emerging patterns of globalization and corporatization. Broadly speaking, the British media is following American patterns in pursuit of American sponsorship. American capital is thereby reproducing the American pattern of decontextualized storytelling.

We find that the British *News at Ten*, with the new initiatives in broadcasting style

> is part of a new-look bulletin, which will, in the words of one ITN executive, become 'more formulaic with a more distinctive human interest approach'. Viewers, it seems, like certainty both in the format of a bulletin and the person who presents it. Lessons have been learnt from American TV news by senior ITN managers, such as chief executive Bob Phillis, editor-in-chief Stewart Purvis, and *News at Ten* producer Nigel Dacre (brother of Paul, the new editor of the *Daily Mail*).

(Brooks 1992: 69)

The reasons for the convergence with American styles of storytelling are addressed later.

> By 1994, ITV companies must become minority shareholders in ITN. American TV companies, CNN, CBS and NBC, have already cast their eyes over ITN, though only one of them is likely to take a stake. It is no

coincidence that *News at Ten* will have a more of an American look –
the single anchor, like Dan Rather or Peter Jennings, for example.

In short, ITN and *News at Ten* are being dressed up to be more
attractive not just to viewers, but also to prospective buyers.

(1992: 69)

In America, it is obvious that the 'story' is being employed specifically to
close off sustained political and cultural analysis. John Simpson wrote about
'the closing of the American media'. In this closure, the 'story' took pride of
place in cutting America off from international news and political analysis.
Simpson analysed the CBS news:

After reports on drought in the Western United States and the day's
domestic political news, the rest of CBS's news broadcast was devoted
to a regular feature, *Eye on America*. This evening's item was about a
man who was cycling across America with his son, a sufferer from
cerebral palsy. It was designed to leave you with a warm feeling, and
lasted for three minutes, 58 seconds; longer than the time devoted that
night to the whole of the rest of the world.

It is no surprise that soon there will almost certainly be no American
television network correspondent based anywhere in the southern
hemisphere. Goodbye Africa; goodbye most of Asia; goodbye Latin
America.

(Simpson 1992: 9)

As you would expect from a Briton, Simpson concludes that the only reposi-
tory of serious cultural analysis is on British television which, as we have
seen, is being restructured according to American imperatives.

The circle, in short, is closed:

The sound of an Englishman being superior about America is rarely
uplifting; but in this case the complaints come most fiercely from the
people who work for American television themselves. They know how
steep the decline has been, and why it has happened. All three networks
have been brought up by giant corporations which appear to regard
news and current affairs as branches of the entertainment industry, and
insist they have to pay their way with advertisers just as chat shows
and sitcoms do. Advertisers are not good people for a news organisation to rely on: during the Gulf war NBC lost $25 million in revenue
because companies which had bought space in the news bulletins
cancelled their advertisements – they were afraid their products would
appear alongside reports of American casualties.

The decline of the networks is depressing. CBS is one of the grandest
names in journalism, the high-minded organisation which broadcast
Ed Murrow's wartime dispatches from London and Walter Cronkite's

influential verdicts on the Vietnam War and Watergate. NBC's record is
a proud one too. Recently it announced it was back in the news business
and would stop broadcasting stories that were simply features. But
NBC News seems very close to the rocks nowadays, and it does
not have the money to send its teams abroad in the way it did until a
couple of years ago. The foreign coverage will mostly be based on
pictures from the British television news agency Visnews, and from
the BBC.

(Simpson 1992: 9)

We have entered the period of 'authoritarian capital', and Simpson
argues that the 'story' is the indicator of this denouement. If this is so, the
promoters of storying have strange bedfellows.

Earl and Irma, meanwhile, are still there in front of their television sets,
serenely unaware of what is happening around them. Decisions which
affect their lives are being taken every day in Frankfurt, Tokyo and
London, but no one tells them about it. Most of the companies which
advertise on television just want them to feel good so, therefore, do the
people in charge of providing them with news. The freest society in the
world has achieved the kind of news blackout which totalitarian
regimes can only dream about.

(1992: 9)

In one sense, the enshrinement of the personal story as a central motif for
knowledge transmission links up with another theme in current restructuring, namely, the reconstruction of the middle ground in the social and
economic system. By sponsoring voices at the periphery, the centre may well
be strengthening its hand. Hence, empowerment of personal and peripheral
voices can go hand-in-hand with aggrandizement and a further concentration of power at the centre, as Alan Wolfe (1989) has pointed out in his
book, *Whose Keeper?*:

A debate that casts government and the marketplace as the main
mechanisms of social organisation leaves out all those intermediate
institutions that are, in fact, the most important in people's lives:
family, church, neighbourhood associations, workplace ties, unions
and a variety of informed organisations.

(Quoted in Dionne 1992: 18)

The current appeal to personal and 'family values' in the US elections,
undoubtedly, is driven by a realization of this kind of dissolution of
mediating social structures:

The appeal of this vague phrase is that fundamentally it reminds
people that good society depends not only, or even primarily, on their

economic well-being, but also on this web of personal–social relationships that transcend the marketplace and transcend government.

(Rosenthal 1992: 1)

This focus on storytelling emerged early in the movies. By 1914, William and Cecil DeMille had developed a technique of storytelling that would 'follow the old dramatic principles, but adapt itself to a new medium . . . find its own compensations for its lack of words . . . to make a train of thought visible enough to be photographed' (Berg 1989: 48). By 1916, this had evolved to the point where a ghostwriter for Samuel Goldwyn could write, 'By the time I started the Goldwyn Company it was the player, not the play which was the thing' (Berg 1989: 68). Likewise, in the world of fantasy promoted by the movies, stories are the central motif for colonizing and redirecting lived experience. This has been so since very early on as the Goldwyn quotes indicate:

> A painless way to make sense of this New World was suggested by one of the modernising forces itself: the movies. The movies offered many forms of guidance to confused Americans, particularly to immigrant urban dwellers; they became a virtual manual for acculturation. But one of the most important and most subtle services the movies offered was to serve as a popular model of narrative coherence. If reality was overwhelming, one could always carve it into a story, as the movies did. One could bend life to the familiar and comforting formulas one saw in the theatre.
>
> (*New York Times* 1991: 32)

From the beginning, movies began to explore new terrains for formularizing and domesticating reality.

In American life, beginning in the 1920s, a number of media began to exploit the storying theme first initiated in the movies. The tabloid press, and then magazines and television, began to provide a range of real-life plots, from kidnappings and murder to political scandals, to crimes in executive suites, to election campaigns, to the Second World War, to the cold war, to Watergate, to the Soviet coup attempt, to 'Operation Restore Hope':

> Today, virtually all the news assumes a narrative configuration with cause and effect, villain and hero, beginning, middle and provisional end, and frequently a moral. Events that don't readily conform, the savings and loan scandal, for example, seem to drift in foggy limbo like a European art film rather than a sleek commercial American hit.
>
> (*New York Times* 1991: 32)

It might be judged that the savings and loan scandal could have been made to conform to a very exciting storyline, but it was in fact pushed off into foggy limbo. This raises the key question of the power of storying to make vivid and realistic certain storylines while suppressing others. It is clear that murders and fires and kidnappings are exciting material for storylines, but that many of the things that go on in American society somehow or other do not form a reasonable storyline. It is interesting, therefore, that so influential a newspaper as the *New York Times* should see the savings and loan scandal as not worthy of a storyline. They are, in short, accepting the assumptions which underpin the genre.

Let me return once more to the *New York Times* for one extended quote on the importance of storying in the news:

> That is why reading the news is just like watching a series of movies: a hostage crisis is a thriller, the Milwaukee serial murders a morbidly fascinating real-life *Silence of the Lambs*, the Kennedy Palm Beach case a soap opera, a fire or hurricane a disaster picture.
>
> One even suspects that Americans were riveted by the Clarence Thomas–Anita Hill hearings last week not because of any sense of civic duty but because it was a spellbinding show – part *Rashomon*, part *Thelma and Louise*, part *Witness for the Prosecution*.
>
> But as with movies, if 'formularizing' reality is a way of domesticating it, it is also a means of escaping it. Michael Wood in his book *America in the Movies*, described our films as a 'rearrangement of our problems into shapes which tame them, which disperse them to the margins of our attention' where we can forget about them. By extending this function to life itself, we convert everything from the kidnapping of the Lindbergh baby to the marital misadventures of Elizabeth Taylor into distractions, cheap entertainments that transport us from our problems. But before disapproving too quickly, one is almost compelled to admit that turning life into escapist entertainment has both a perverse logic and a peculiar genius. Why worry about the seemingly intractable problems of society when you can simply declare, 'It's morning in America' and have yourself a long-running Frank Capra movie right down to an aw-shucks President? Why fret over America's declining economic might when you can have an honest-to-goodness war movie that proves your superiority? Movies have always been a form of wish fulfilment. Why not life?
>
> When life is a movie, it poses serious questions for those things that were not traditionally entertainment and now must accommodate themselves. Politics, for instance. Much has already been made of the fact that Ronald Reagan came to the White House after a lifetime as a professional actor. Lou Cannon, in his biography of Mr Reagan, *President Reagan: The Role of a Lifetime*, details just how central this

was to Mr Reagan's concept of the Presidency and what it suggests about the political landscape.

(New York Times 1991: 32)

The important point to grasp about this quote and other quotes is that the storying genre is far from socially and politically neutral. As we saw in an earlier quotation, the savings and loan scandal was somehow not a valid storyline. Likewise, the great exploiters of storylines – the John Waynes, the Ronald Reagans – tend to be of a particular political persuasion and of a particular sensitivity to the dominant interest groups within American society. Storying, therefore, rapidly becomes a form of social and political prioritizing; a particular way of telling stories which, in its way, privileges some storylines and silences others. Once the focus shifts, not to real events but 'what makes a good story', it is a short distance to making an argument that certain political realities 'would not make a good story' while others would. By displacing its focus from real-life events into storying potential, it is possible also to displace some unwanted social and political realities. Even when unwanted realities do intrude in deafening ways, such as the LA riots, it is possible to story them in ways that create a distance of sorts. In Umberto Eco's words, it is possible to move from a situation where realities are scrutinized and analysed to the world of American life where 'hyper-realities' are constructed (Eco 1986).

Storytelling and educational study

Now, although the use of stories by the media to close off political and cultural analysis does not itself disprove the value of storying and narrative in educational study, I would, however, urge that it is cause for thought in two ways. First, if stories are so easily used in this manner in the media, it is plainly possible that they might act in this way as educational study. Secondly, as is made clear in some of the foregoing quotes, the way we 'story' our lives (and, therefore, the way we present ourselves for educational study, among other things) is deeply connected to storylines derived from elsewhere. In American life especially, but increasingly elsewhere, forms of narrative and storying, the classic 'storylines', are often derived from television and newspapers. In this sense, Ronald Reagan is not alone; he made such a representative President because of his capacity to catch and dispatch the central storylines of American life. 'It's morning in America' as a campaign slogan sounded right and true. It was a powerful storyline and it was not seriously contested by political or cultural analysis.

Stories, then, need to be closely interrogated and analysed in their social context. Stories, in short, are most often carriers of dominant messages, themselves agencies of domination. Oppositional stories can be captured, but they are very much in the minority and are often themselves overlaid or reactive to dominant storylines. As Gordon Wells has warned us, a previous expression of reality is largely

> a distillation of the stories that we have shared: not only the narratives that we have heard and told, read, or seen enacted in drama or news on television, but also the anecdotes, explanations, and conjectures that are drawn upon in everyday conversation.
>
> (Wells 1986: 196)

Or as Passerini (1987: 28) noted, 'when someone is asked for his life-story, his memory draws on pre-existing story-lines and ways of telling stories, even if these are in part modified by the circumstances'. Put another way, this means that we often narrate our lives according to a 'prior script', a script written elsewhere, by others, for other purposes.

Seen in this way, the use of stories in educational study needs to become part of a broader project of reappropriation. It is not sufficient to say we wanted 'to listen to people', 'to capture their voices', 'to let them tell their stories'. A far more active collaboration is required. Luisa Passerini's work on the Turin's working class and on women's personal narratives is exemplary in this regard (Passerini 1987, 1989). As Weiler has summarized:

> Passerini's emphasis on recurrent narrative forms begins to uncover the way people reconcile contradictions, the ways they create meaning from their lives, and create a coherent sense of themselves through available forms of discourse. At the same time, she is concerned with the 'bad fit' or 'gap' between 'preexisting story lines' and individual constructions of the self through memory. As individuals construct their past, they leave unresolved contradictions at precisely those points at which authoritative discourse conflicts with collective cultural meanings.
>
> (Weiler 1991: 6–7)

At the centre of any move to aid people, and teachers in particular, to reappropriate their individual lived experiences as stories, is the need for active collaboration. In the case of teachers, this will sometimes be in association with educators located in the academy, especially in faculties of education.

The relationship of studies of teachers' stories to the academy sits, I believe, at the centre of one of the major ethical and methodological issues involved in any move to develop collaborative use of stories. Of course, views of the academy cover a wide spectrum, from a belief in its role in the 'disinterested pursuit of knowledge' through to the 1968 *Situationist International* assertion that 'the intelligentsia is power's hall of mirrors'. In general, I would take a position which stresses the *interestedness* rather than disinterestedness of the academy. I see a good deal of empirical evidence that David Tripp's contention in this matter may be correct for he argues that 'when a research method gains currency and academic legitimacy, it tends to be transformed to serve the interests of the academy' (Tripp 1987: 2).

Howard Becker has commented on the 'hierarchy of credibility regarding those to whom we tend to listen'. This has general relevance to our research on schooling and school systems, and specifically to our desire to listen to the teacher's voice:

> In any system of ranked groups, participants take it as given that members of the highest group have the right to define the way things really are. In any organisation, no matter what the rest of the organisa-tion chart shows, the arrows indicate the flow of information point up, thus demonstrating (at least formally) that those at the top have access to a more complete picture of what is going on than anyone else. Mem-bers of lower groups will have incomplete information and their view of reality will be partial and distorted in consequence. Therefore, from the point of view of a well-socialised participant in the system, any tale told by those at the top intrinsically deserves to be regarded as the most credible account obtainable of the organisation's workings.
>
> (Becker 1970: 126)

Becker provides a particular reason why accounts 'from below' may be unwelcome:

> Officials usually have to lie. That is a gross way of putting it, but not inaccurate. Officials must lie because things are seldom as they ought to be. For a great variety of reasons, well known to sociologists, institu-tions are refractory. They do not perform as society would like them to. Hospitals do not cure people; prisons do not rehabilitate prisoners; schools do not educate students. Since they are supposed to, officials develop ways both of denying the failure of the institution to perform as it should and explaining those failures which cannot be hidden. An account of an institution's operation from the point of view of sub-ordinates therefore casts doubt on the official line and may possibly expose it as a lie.
>
> (1970: 128)

For these reasons, the academy normally accepts the

> hierarchy of credibility . . . we join officials and the man in the street in an unthinking acceptance of the hierarchy of credibility. We do not realise that there are sides to be taken and that we are taking one of them.
>
> (1970: 129)

Hence, Becker argues that for the academic researcher:

> The hierarchy of credibility is a feature of society whose existence we cannot deny, even if we disagree with its injunction to believe the man at the top. When we acquire sufficient sympathy with subordinates to see things from their perspective, we know that we are flying in the face of what 'everyone knows'. The knowledge gives us pause and causes us to share, however briefly, the doubt of our colleagues.
>
> (1970: 129)

Research work, then, is seldom disinterested, and prime interests at work are the powerful Becker's 'man at the top' (*sic*) and the academy itself. Acknowledgement of these interests becomes crucial when we conduct studies of teachers' stories, for the data generated and accounts rendered can easily be misused and abused by both powerful interest groups and by the academy. Middleton (1992: 20) notes that 'in schools people are constantly regulated and classified', but this surveillance extends to teachers themselves. Plainly, studies of teachers' stories can be implicated in this process unless we are deeply watchful about who 'owns' the data and who controls the accounts. If Becker is right that 'officials lie', it is also plain that they might appropriate and misuse data about teachers' lives. Likewise, those in the academy might take information on teachers' lives and use it entirely for their own purposes.

Yet Becker reminds us that the terrain of research involves not only differentiated voices but also stratified voices. It is important to remember that the politicians and bureaucrats who control schools are part of a stratified system where 'those at the top have a more complete picture of what is going on than anyone else' (Becker 1970: 126). It would be unfortunate if, in studying teachers' stories, we ignored these contextual parameters which so substantially impinge upon and constantly restrict the teacher's life. It is, therefore, I think, a crucial part of our ethical position as researchers that we do not 'valorise the subjectivity of the powerless' in the name of telling 'their story' (Denzin 1992: 2). This would be merely to record constrained consciousness – a profoundly conservative posture and one, as Denzin (1992) has noted, that explains the popularity of such work during the most recent conservative political renaissance. In my view, teachers' stories should, where possible, provide not only a *narrative of action*, but also a history of *genealogy of context*. I say this in the full knowledge that this opens up substantial dangers of changing the relationship between 'story giver' and 'research taker', and of tilting the balance of the relationship further towards the academy.

I think, however, that these dangers must be faced if a genuine collaboration between the life story giver and the research taker is to be achieved. In a real sense, *it cannot be all give and no take*. In what sense is the 'research taker' in a position to give and provide the basis for a reasonably equitable collaboration? I have argued elsewhere (Goodson and Fliesser 1994) that what we are searching for in developing genuine collaboration in studying teachers' stories is a viable *trading point* between life story giver and research taker. The key to this trading point is, I believe, the differential structural location of the researcher. The academic has the time and the resources to collaborate with teachers in developing *genealogies of context*. These genealogies can provide teachers as a group with aspects of 'the complete picture', which those that control their lives have (or at least aspire to have):

> Much of the work that is emerging on teachers' lives throws up structural insights which locate the teacher's life within the deeply structured and embedded environment of schooling. This provides a prime 'trading point' for the external researcher. For one of the valuable characteristics of a collaboration between teachers as researchers and external researchers is that it is a collaboration between two parties that are differentially located in structural terms. Each sees the world through a different prism of practice and thought. This valuable difference may provide the external researcher with a possibility to offer back goods in 'the trade'. The teacher/researcher offers data and insights. The terms of trade, in short, look favourable. In such conditions collaboration may at last begin.
>
> (Goodson and Walker 1991: 148–9)

In arguing for the provision of histories or genealogies of context, I am reminded of V.S. Naipaul's comments. Naipaul (1988) has the ultimate sensitivity to the 'stories' that people tell about their lives; for him subjective perceptions are priority data. Buruma has judged:

> What makes Naipaul one of the world's most civilised writers is his refusal to be engaged by the People, and his insistence on listening to people, individuals, with their own language and their own stories. To this extent he is right when he claims to have no view; he is impatient with abstractions. He is interested in how individual people see themselves and the world in which they live. He has recorded their histories, their dreams, their stories, their words.
>
> (Buruma 1991: 3)

So far, then, Naipaul echoes the concern of those educational researchers who have sought to capture teachers' stories and narratives, told in their own words and in their own terms. But I am interested by the more recent shifts in Naipaul's position: he has begun to provide far more historical background; he seems to me to be moving towards providing the stories, but also genealogies of context. He is clear that he sees this as empowering those whose stories which he once told more passively, 'to awaken to history was to cease to live instinctively. It was to begin to see oneself and one's group the way the outside world saw one; and it was to know a kind of rage' (quoted in Buruma 1991: 4).

MacIntyre has followed a similar line in arguing that man is 'essentially a storytelling animal'. He argues:

> The story of my life is always embedded in the story of those communities from which I derive my identity. What I am, therefore, is in key part what I inherit, a specific past that is present to some degree in my present. I find myself part of a history and that is generally to say, whether I like it or not, whether I recognise it or not, one of the bearers of a tradition. It was important when I characterised the concept of a practice to notice that practices always have histories and that at any given moment what a practice is depends on a mode of understanding it which has been transmitted often through many generations. And thus, insofar as the virtues sustain the relationships required for practices, they have to sustain relationships to the past – and to the future – as well as in the present. But the traditions through which particular practices are transmitted and reshaped never exist in isolation for larger social traditions.
>
> (MacIntyre 1981: 206–7)

MacIntyre continues:

> Within a tradition the pursuit of goods extends through generations, sometimes through many generations. Hence the individual's search for his or her good is generally and characteristically conducted within a context defined by those traditions of which the individual's life is a part, and this is true both of those goods which are internal to practices and of the goods of a single life. Once again the narrative phenomenon of embedding is crucial: the history of a practice in our time is generally and characteristically embedded in and made intelligible in terms of the larger and longer history of the tradition through which the practice in its present form was conveyed to us; the history of each of our own lives is generally and characteristically embedded in and made intelligible in terms of the larger and longer histories of a number of traditions.
>
> (1981: 206–7)

In many ways, Middleton summarizes the aspirations when she says:

> Teachers, as well as their students, should analyse the relationship between their individual biographies, historical events, and the constraints imposed on their personal choices by broader power relations, such as those of class, race and gender.
>
> (Middleton 1992: 19)

In providing such intercontextual analysis, the different methodologies highlighted in this volume all provide important avenues. They all combine a concern with telling teachers' stories with an equal concern to provide a broader context for the location, understanding and grounding of those stories.

In awakening to history in our studies of teachers' stories, I have felt for some time that life history work is a most valuable avenue for collaborative, intercontextual work (Goodson 1992; Goodson and Sikes 2001). The distinction between life stories and life histories is an important one to restate. The life story is a personal reconstruction of experience, in this case by the teacher. Life story givers provide data for the researcher, often in loosely structured interviews. The researcher seeks to elicit the teacher's perceptions and stories but is generally passive rather than actively interrogative.

The life history also begins with the life story that the teacher tells, but seeks to build on the information provided. Hence other people's accounts might be elicited, documentary evidence and a range of historical data amassed. The concern is to develop a wide intertextual and intercontextual mode of analysis. This provision of a wider range of data allows a contextual background to be constructed.

Crucial to the move to life history is a change in the nature of collaboration. The teacher becomes more than a teller of stories and becomes a more general investigator; the external researcher is more than a listener and elicitor of stories, and is actively involved in textual and contextual construction. In terms of give and take, I would argue a more viable trading point could be established. This trading point, by focusing on stories *in context*, provides a new focus to develop our joint understandings of schooling. By providing this dialogue of a *story of action within a theory of context*, a new context is provided for collaboration. In the end, the teacher as researcher can collaborate in investigating not only the stories of lives but also the contexts of lives. Such collaboration should provide new understandings for all of us concerned with the world of schooling.

Personal knowledge and educational research

As we have seen, storytelling has been a sign in the media of a move away from cultural and political analysis. Why, then, might we assume that it would be any different in educational and social research? After all, educational research has tended to be behind mainstream cultural and political analysis in its cogency and vitality rather than ahead of it. Let us go back a step. Storytelling came in because the modes of cultural and political analysis were biased, white, male and middle-class. Other ways of knowing and representing grew at the periphery of research to challenge the biased centre.

However, these oppositional discourses, having achieved some success in representing 'silenced voices', have remained ensconced in the particular and the specific. They have, in short, not developed their own linkages to cultural, political analysis.

The assumption of so much postmodernist optimism is that by empowering new voices and discourses, by telling stories, we will rewrite and reinscribe the old white male bourgeois rhetoric, and so it may be. But so what? New stories do not of themselves analyse or address the structures of power. Is it not the commonsensical level, worthy of pause, to set the new stories and new voices against a sense of the centre's continuing power? The Western version of high modernity is everywhere ascendant. We have an unparalleled *end of history triumphalism* with most of the historical challenges vanquished. Is this new ascendant authoritarian global power a likely vehicle for the empowerment of the silenced and the oppressed? This seems unlikely, particularly since such power has historically been the vehicle for the very construction and silencing of the same oppressed groups. Is it not more likely, then, that new discourses and voices that empower the periphery at one and the same time fortify, enhance and solidify the old centres of power? In short, are we not witnessing the old game of divide and rule?

The collection of stories, then, especially the mainstream stories that live out a 'prior script', will merely fortify patterns of domination. We need to move from life stories to life histories, from narratives to genealogies of context, towards a modality that embraces *stories of action within theories of context*. In so doing, stories can be 'located', seen as the social constructions they are, fully impregnated by their location within power structures and social milieux. Stories provide a starting point for active collaboration, 'a process of deconstructing the discursive practices through which one's subjectivity has been constituted' (Middleton 1992: 20). Only if we deal with stories as the *starting point* for collaboration, as the *beginning* of a process of coming to know, will we come to understand their meaning; to see them as social constructions which allow us to locate and interrogate the social world in which they are embedded (Goodson and Sikes 2001).

Our studies of the wider uses that stories are put to in the media should warn those of us involved in educational studies that stories can be as easily employed for closure as for exposure. The way we employ storied material, therefore, needs to be painstakingly scrutinized to ensure that issues of social context and construction are fully elucidated. Without this dimension, stories can be a route to social closure, a form of 'dumbing down' all too readily evidenced in the media.

five

Developing life and work histories of teachers

Although there has been spasmodic interest over the last century, life history studies of teachers have remained a sadly neglected genre until recently. There have, however, always been exceptions, and in some cultures, for example Japan, a long tradition of teacher autobiographies has provided valuable data for those involved in life history work. The general neglect of the teacher in educational study has been summarized by Lortie. While these were very different economic and social times, his judgement stands up well today:

> Schooling is long on prescription, short on description. That is nowhere more evident than in the case of the two million persons who teach in the public schools. It is widely conceded that the core transactions of formal education take place where teachers and students meet . . . But although books and articles instructing teachers on how they should behave are legion, empirical studies of teaching work – and the outlook of those who staff the schools – remain rare.
>
> (Lortie 1975: vii)

A conference in the early 1980s at St Hilda's in Oxford, attended by leading American and European researchers, addressed the theme of teachers' lives. In the book produced from the conference, *Teachers' Lives and Careers*, Stephen Ball and Ivor Goodson (1985) argued that British research on teachers had moved through a number of contemporary phases in the last forty years. At the beginning of this period, in the 1960s,

> teachers were shadowy figures on the educational landscape mainly known, or unknown, through large scale surveys or historical analyses

of their position in society, the key concept in approaching the practice of the teaching was that of role.

(Ball and Goodson 1985: 6)

Thus, in this decade, in most research studies, teachers were present in aggregate through imprecise statistics, or were viewed as individuals only as formal role incumbents, mechanistically and unproblematically responding to the powerful expectations of their role set.

As we moved to the late 1960s and early 1970s, new approaches were well underway which began to address some of the limitations of these paradigms. Case study researchers began to scrutinize schooling as a social process, focusing their work on the manner in which school pupils were 'processed':

> The sympathies of the researchers lay primarily with the pupils, working class and female pupils in particular, who were the 'under dogs' in the classroom, teachers were the 'villains of the piece'.
>
> (Ball and Goodson 1985: 7)

By the 1980s, we saw a further shift where attention began to be directed 'to the constraints within which teachers work . . . Teachers were transformed from villains to "victims" and in some cases, "dupes" of the system within which they were required to operate' (1985: 7).

The latter characterization of teachers opened up the question of 'how teachers saw their work and their lives'. By this time, I was developing an explicit argument for the use of life history methods in studying teachers. Writing in 1981, I argued that researchers had not confronted the complexity of the school teacher as an active agent making his or her own history. Researchers, even when they had stopped treating the teacher as a numerical aggregate, historical footnote or unproblematic role incumbent, still treated teachers as interchangeable types unchanged by circumstance or time. As a result, new research methods were needed:

> The pursuit of personal and biographical data might rapidly challenge the assumption of interchangeability. Likewise, by tracing the teacher's life as it evolved over time – throughout the teacher's career and through several generations – the assumption of timelessness might also be remedied. *In understanding something so intensely personal as teaching it is critical we know about the person the teacher is.* Our paucity of knowledge in this area is a manifest indictment of the range of our sociological imagination. The life historian pursues the job from his [*sic*] own perspective, a perspective which emphasises the value of the person's 'own story'.
>
> (Goodson 1981: 69)

While studies of teachers' lives and careers now began to be more generally pursued in the educational research community, unfortunately political and economic changes were moving sharply in the opposite direction and this acted to reverse, at least for a time, the move towards more life history studies. The development of patterns of political and administrative control over teachers has become enormous between the 1980s and the new millennium. In terms of power and visibility, in many ways this represents 'a return to the shadows' for teachers in the face of new curriculum guidelines (in some countries like New Zealand and Britain, an all-encompassing national curriculum); teacher assessment and accountability; a barrage of new policy edicts, and new patterns of school governance and administration. Cochran-Smith and Lytle lay out the educational climate of standards and accountability in the Introduction. They argue that the standards movement 'de-emphasises the construction of local knowledge in and by school communities, and de-emphasises the role of the teacher as decision maker and change agent' (Cochran-Smith and Lytle 1999: 22). A singular focus on 'practice' and 'practical knowledge' accompanies these changing patterns of educational governance.

Obviously, moves that de-emphasise the teacher's agency at the same time deter research workers from focusing on teachers' lives.

New directions for studying the life and work of teaching

In spite of the attack on teachers' agency, recently a new range of contemporary work by qualitative researchers suggests innovative and interesting ways to address the goal of understanding teachers' *personal knowledge* (see Kridel 1998; Denzin and Lincoln 2000; Goodson and Sikes 2001; Roberts 2002). The addition of the personal aspect in this formulation is a positive development, hinting, as it does, at the importance of biographical and personal perspectives.

Other traditions have focused on the reflective practitioner, on teachers-as-researchers of their own practice, and on phenomenological approaches to practice. In these genres, personal experiences are linked irrevocably to practice. It is as if the teacher *is* her or his practice. The 'teacher-as-researcher' approach suggests a number of problems. Stressing that the teacher becomes the researcher of his or her own practice appears to free the researcher in the academy from clear responsibility in this process. In my view, such researchers have a primary but somewhat neglected responsibility for sponsoring and sustaining the teacher-as-researcher. Hence, new traditions are developing which oppose the notion that the focus of the teacher-as-researcher should be mainly upon practice. For teacher educators such specificity of focus is understandable, but broader perspectives might achieve even more, not solely in terms of understandings but ultimately in ways that feed back into changes in practical knowledge, public policy, and infinitely broader theoretical understandings.

The danger with a focus on personal and practical knowledge is that it can rupture the links to theoretical and contextual knowledge. Only if these new modes link to wider narratives about social change and globalization will teachers' knowledge become fully generative and socially and politically efficacious. As Hargreaves has argued, the challenge for postmodern educational research is:

> to connect the localised narratives of students, teachers and parents within their own schools, to the big pictures or grand narratives of educational and social change that are taking place 'out there' beyond their classroom walls, in ways that directly affect their lives behind them.
>
> (Hargreaves 1999: 341)

The daily work of teachers is politically and socially constructed. The parameters of what constitutes practice, whether biographical or political, range over a wide terrain. To narrow the focus to 'practice-as-defined' is to make the focus of research a victim of historical circumstances, particularly political forces. In many ways, 'the forces of the market', as articulated by many politicians, are often having the effect of turning the teacher's practice into that of a routinized and trivialized deliverer of a predesigned package. To accept those definitions and to focus on 'practice' so defined is tantamount to accepting this ideology. By focusing on practice in a narrow way, the initiative for defining the research agenda passes to politicians and bureaucrats. Far more autonomous and critical research will be generated if the research community insist on a broader, more contextual focus. We need above all to move well beyond the grasp of what I have called earlier the 'practical fundamentalists' (Goodson 1995a: 145), but as we see there are dangers within more 'friendly' discourses that have sought to sponsor teacher-based research.

The new traditions that seek to broaden the focus of work with teachers range from life history and biographical studies (Goodson 1981, 1992, 1995b; Goodson and Walker 1991; Tierney 1998, 2000; Roberts 2002), to collaborative biography (Butt *et al.* 1992; Fine 1994), to teachers' professional and micro-political knowledge (Russell and Munby 1992; Goodson and Cole 1993; Goodson and Hargreaves 1996), through a wide range of interesting and innovative feminist work (Acker 1989, 1994; Smith 1990; Dehli 1994; Munro 1998). This work seeks to broaden the focus of teacher education and development, to include the social and political, the contextual and the collective.

A major aspiration of life history studies is to broaden the focus of work with teachers. Such work might take the 'teacher-as-researcher' and 'action research' modes as valuable entry points, but it moves to extend the immediate focus on practice and on individual classrooms. Life history work is *par excellence* qualitative work. The pioneering work of Thomas and Znaniecki (1918–1920) and other proponents at the Chicago School in the 1920s and 1930s is part of the qualitative legacy. Subsequent work, notably by Dollard (1949) and Klockars (1975), has continued the tradition of American scholarship. In Britain, the work of Paul Thompson (1988; Thompson *et al.* 1991) and his use of life histories to study ageing has continued to rehabilitate and develop the life history tradition, as has the work of Ken Plummer (2001).

In teacher education and teacher development, much pioneering work has been undertaken. The work of Sikes *et al.* (1985) and Goodson and Sikes (2001) is helpful in developing our understanding of teachers' careers, as is the study *Teachers' Lives and Careers* (Ball and Goodson 1985). The study by Hargreaves (1994) adds a valuable contextual commentary to our understanding of the enormous global changes that are affecting the life and work of teachers, so also does Hargreaves's new work on the emotional dimensions of teaching (Hargreaves 1998, 2001). Sandra Acker's work is also illuminative of the gender issues embedded in teachers' lives and careers (Acker 1989, 1999).

Martin Lawn (1990) has written powerfully about teachers' biographies and of how teachers' work has been rapidly restructured in England and Wales. Bullough's work (1989, 1998; Bullough *et al.* 1991) has begun to tell us a great deal about the process of becoming a teacher. Michael Huberman (1993) brings a social psychological tint to his work on teachers' life histories, and also in his recent work has provided considerable methodological insight and illumination (Huberman *et al.* 1997).

Likewise, Susan Robertson (1994, 1996, 1997) has analysed teachers' work in the context of post-fordist economies. She argues that again teachers' professionalism has been drastically reconstructed and replaced by a wholly 'new professionalism'.

Such major restructuration of the work life of teachers highlights the limitations of those methods which focus on the practical and personal worlds of teachers and are limited to story and narrative modes. Teachers' personal and practical reminiscences and commentaries relate to their work and practice. So such data, in the new domain described by Lawn and Robertson, will be primarily about work where moral and professional judgement plays less and less of a part. By focusing on the personal and practical, teacher data and stories are encouraged which forego the chance to speak of other ways, other people, other times and other forms of being a teacher. The focus of research methods solely on the personal and practical is then an act of methodological abdication, of the right to speak on matters of social and political construction. By speaking in this voice about personal and practical matters, the researcher and teacher both lose a voice in the moment of speaking. For the voice that has been encouraged and granted space in the public domain, in the realm of personal and practical, is the voice of technical competency, the voice of the isolated classroom practitioner, the voices of workers whose work has been restructured and reconstructed.

By using life history methods in studying teachers' life and work in a fuller social context, the intention is to develop insights often in a grounded and collaborative manner into the social construction of teaching. In this way, teachers' stories of action can be reconnected with 'histories of context'. Hence teaching stories, rather than passively celebrating the continual reconstruction of teaching, will move to develop understandings of social and political construction. It is the move from commentary on what *is* to cognition of what *might be*, or, to use Shotter's terms, from the enlightenment mode of rational order towards something he calls the 'imaginary' (Shotter 1993: 199).

Life history studies of the teacher's life and work as social construction provide a valuable lens for observing contemporary moves to restructure and reform schooling. Butt *et al.* have talked about the 'crisis of reform', when so much of the restructuring and reformist initiatives depend on prescriptions imported into the classroom but are developed as political imperatives elsewhere. These patterns of intervention develop from a particular view of the teacher, a view which practical genres of study often work to confirm:

> All their lives teachers have to confront the negative stereotypes – 'teacher as robot, devil, angel, nervous Nellie' – foisted upon them by the American culture. Descriptions of teaching as a 'flat occupation with no career structure, low pay, salary increments unrelated to merit' have been paralleled with portrayals of teaching as 'one great plateau' where 'it appears that the annual cycle of the school year lulls teachers into a repetitious professional cycle of their own'.
>
> Within the educational community, the image of teachers as semi-professionals who lack control and autonomy over their own work and as persons who do not contribute to the creation of knowledge has permeated and congealed the whole educational enterprise. Researchers have torn the teacher out of the context of classroom, plagued her with various insidious effects (Hawthorne, novelty, Rosenthal, halo), parcelled out into discrete skills the unity of intention and action present in teaching practices.
>
> (Butt *et al.* 1992: 55)

In some ways, the crisis of reform is a crisis of prescriptive optimism – a belief that what is politically pronounced and backed with armouries of accountability tests will actually happen. But the data which will challenge these simplifications, data rooted in the teacher's life and work, will have to move beyond the currently popular 'practical' viewpoints to develop a broader counter-culture of commentary which is focused on the everyday life and work of the teacher, student and school.

The value(s) of studies of work and life

A major value underpinning studies of teachers' work and lives is that such studies increase the visibility and indeed usability of teachers' perspectives. In many of the educational changes and reforms currently being undertaken with accelerating speed around the world, teachers' perspectives are too often missing. Hence, research studies of teachers' work and lives provide a powerful antidote to such wilful obfuscation. By focusing on teachers' work and life histories, a wide range of different perspectives will be provided about new moves to reform, restructure and reconceptualize schooling. All too commonly, the new prescriptions and educational changes that are being legislated work against the history and context of the teacher's work and life. By not considering these teacher perspectives, it is likely that a new crisis of change and reform will be generated. For, all too clearly, if teachers are not fully considered in the new initiatives, their centrality in the process will 'act back' against the very essence of the reforms.

One good example of this is provided in Casey's study published in 1992. Her work provides an illustration of how studying teachers' lives can illuminate a range of practical reform problems: in this case, the issue of 'teacher dropout'. She shows how a certain framework of taken-for-granted assumptions have pervaded the way in which the problem of teacher attrition has normally been defined. The definition presumes managerial solutions, and this presumption is confirmed in the discourse which arises from management in phrases like 'teacher defection', 'supply and demand' and 'teacher turnover'. By focusing managerially, the question of teacher dropout is essentially obscured. Casey shows how, in studying the problem, teacher dropout has been largely looked at statistically rather than in person, and that information has typically been collected from sources such as state departments of public instruction or district files, or through researcher-dominated surveys. As she points out, these strategies too often work with the grain of power/knowledge as it is held by management and bureaucratic elites in the educational system. Casey argues:

> The particular configuration of selectivities and omissions which has been built into this research frame slants the shape of its findings. By systematically failing to record the voices of ordinary teachers, the

literature on educators' careers actually silences them. Methodologic-ally, this means that even while investigating an issue where decision-making is paramount, researchers speculate on teachers' motivations, or at best, survey them with a set of forced-choice options. Theoretic-ally, what emerges is an instrumental view of teachers, one in which they are reduced to objects which can be manipulated for particular ends. Politically, the results are educational policies constructed around institutionally convenient systems of rewards and punishments, rather than in congruence with teachers' desires to create significance in their lives.

(Casey 1992: 188)

The vital importance of teachers' life and work testimonies is that they expose the shallowness, not to say inaccuracy of the managerial, prescriptive view of school change. A further advantage of studies in life and work is the insights that are provided on the question of teacher socialization. An underpinning belief in much of the literature on teacher socialization has defined the period of pre-service teacher training and the early phases of in-service training as the prime formative socializing influences on styles of teaching. There is, however, an alternative research tradition developed from life and work studies which points to a far more complex progress at work. Many studies from the 1960s onwards have focused on the teacher's own experience as a pupil. In his study, *Schoolteacher*, Dan Lortie (1975) has referred to this pupil period as an 'apprenticeship of observation' where the would-be teacher internalizes many future role possibilities. Teacher socialization in this tradition occurs through the observation and internal-ization of models of teaching. Lortie argues that these models, which he calls 'latent models', are activated but not implanted during the training period, having often been 'carried in suspension through the interim period of time'. To explore this alternative conceptualization in teacher socialization requires that we do far more life history work covering the pattern of socialization of teachers over the full span of their work and life in teaching.

Teacher life and work histories also allow considerable elucidation of gender perspectives. This work has been pursued in interesting ways by feminist scholars, such as Sandra Acker (1989, 1994, 1999), Sue Middleton (1992, 1993, 1997) and Munro (1998). Their studies and other feminist work provide vital and insightful perspectives into teaching as a gendered profession. For instance, the work of Margaret Nelson has sought to reconstruct the work experiences of women teachers in Vermont in the early twentieth century. She notes:

Numerous studies have shown that there is a gap between what we can discover when we rely on published accounts of some historical event and what we can discover when we ask questions of the on-site participants of those same events. This gap looms larger when we are looking at women's history because of the private nature of so much of women's lives.

(Nelson 1992: 168)

In general, life history studies of teaching aid the production of a wider range of teacher-centred professional knowledge. To move educational study in this direction requires a major upheaval and reconceptualizing of existing educational research paradigms. Nonetheless, the emerging work from a range of genres, from teacher journalling through to teacher thinking, through to work on teachers' practical and professional knowledge, as well as the emerging studies of reflective practitioners and action-researchers, is a solid baseline for such a newly conceptualized mode of educational research. In this sense, life history studies of their nature insist that understanding teacher agency is a vital part of educational research and one that we ignore at our peril.

Studying teachers' lives and careers

This is a difficult and, in some senses, a dangerous time to be promoting studies of the teacher's life and work. Such studies are both potentially enormously useful in elucidating our understandings of the teacher's work life, and also deeply amenable to misuse by some of the forces currently advocating the restructuration of schooling. In favour of studies of the teacher's life and work is the belief that, by building our knowledge of teachers' perspectives, we can interrogate the experience and reform of schooling in helpful ways. The teacher is a central agent in the delivery of all versions of schooling, and the disavowal of teacher perspectives is a worrying feature of a good deal of recent change and reform. Hence, by studying the teacher's life and work, it is hoped to redress this imbalance.

Against the study of teachers' lives is the considerable potential for misuse by those administering and seeking to restructure schooling. Understanding and, indeed, surveillance of the teacher's life and work could be of immeasurable use in defining and promoting reforms which in many ways are antithetical to many teacher perspectives. For instance, some of the new battery of tests and accountability devices might be seen in this light. Knowing more about the teacher's life and work and integrating these perspectives into reforms can be presented as developing new 'ownership' for the teacher or, in less subtle terms, as 'professional or human resource development strategies'. The new discourse of sensitivity to the identities of the teacher/deliverer of other people's intentions is part of the general marketization and co-modification of the professions.

This Janus-faced aspect of the study of teachers' lives makes it imperative that we think very carefully about the ethical procedures and patterns of disclosure (and anonymity) which are associated with this kind of work. My view is that these questions of ethics and data ownership are *always* central to work on life histories and personal perspectives. It is true that the current period is a time for extreme sensitivity in this regard, but it is always the case that personal data can be misused by administrative and political interests and, therefore, it is both a timeless and timely issue.

A good deal of postmodern and feminist writing has been deeply thoughtful about these matters and has begun to provide a number of useful ways forward. However, it is important to be cognizant of the fact that the 'colonizing' aspect of all work on teachers' lives is not confined to the administrative and political, but also to our own work as researchers. As we saw earlier in the chapter, this has led to some work on teachers' personal, practical knowledge which confines the researcher to the role of 'scribe', recording in faithful and exact form the teacher's voice and limiting commentary to a minimum. While cognizant of the dangers of a more authorial position, it is important to seek some thematic and contextual understanding of the personal data which is elicited from studies of teachers' life and work histories.

In the following section a number of such themes and concepts are delineated and these may seem too logical and, indeed, linear for some postmodern fashions. They may, for example, be seen as presenting a desire for 'closure and coherence' of the sort that is far too painstaking for the disparate, diverse and dissolving aspects of lives in teaching.

Although there are aspects of 'closure', in the way that accounts and representations are made of the teacher's life and work, this is not the central site of 'closure'. Much as we academics may wish to believe in the centrality of our work, no teachers' lives are subject to degrees of 'closure', largely because they take place in one of the most historically circumscribed of political and social spaces. Increasingly, as we have seen, schools are now subjected to a battery of government regulations, edicts, tests, curricula, assessments and accountabilities. It is in this domain that the perimeters for teacher agency are both patrolled and controlled. Hence, it is in this domain where 'closure' is most evident and needs to be most carefully monitored and witnessed.

Given this historical circumscription, we find ourselves unable to follow postmodern fashion in seeing teachers as having selves that are multiple, disparate and free-floating, subject to constant change and flux. Such a vision of the possibilities of teacher agency ignores the socialized and circumscribed spaces and trajectories of the teacher's life and work. By focusing our study on teachers' life and work histories in these closely patrolled institutional venues, the intention, far from seeking academic 'closure', is on the contrary to create vital spaces for reflexivity and commentary. The work aims to develop our strategies for teachers to reflect upon and analyse their life and work in teaching, in ways that allow a more profound and powerful response to the socially constructed world of schooling.

In arguing for an extended range of studies of teachers' life and work histories, I listed a number of conceptual foci for such work (Goodson 1991).

Life experiences and background are obviously key ingredients of the person that we are – of our sense of self – to the degree that we invest our 'self' in our teaching; experience and background therefore shape our practice.

A common feature in many teachers' accounts of their background is the appearance of a favourite teacher who substantially influenced the person as a young school pupil. They often report that 'it was this person who first sold me on teaching'; 'it was sitting in her classroom when I first decided I wanted to be a teacher'. In short, such people provide a 'role model' and, in addition, they most probably influence the subsequent vision of desirable pedagogy as well as, possibly, choice of subject specialism.

Many other ingredients of background are important in the teacher's life and practice. An upbringing in a working-class environment may, for instance, provide valuable insights and experience when teaching pupils from a similar background. I once observed a teacher with a working-class background teach a class of comprehensive pupils in a school in the East End of London. He taught using the local cockney vernacular and his affinity was a quite startling aspect of his success as a teacher. In my interview, I spoke about his affinity and he noted that it was ' 'cos I come from round 'ere don't I?' Background and life experience were then a major aspect of his practice, but so they would be in the case of middle-class teachers teaching children from the working class, or teachers of working-class origins teaching middle-class children. Background is an important ingredient in the dynamic of practice (see Lortie 1975; Munro 1998).

Of course, while class is just one aspect, as are gender or ethnicity, of more general patternings, teachers' backgrounds and life experiences are idiosyncratic and unique and must be explored therefore in their full complexity. Treatment of gender issues has often been historically and sociologically inadequate (Sikes *et al.* 1985). A growing body of work seeks to redress this inadequacy (Smith 1990; Casey 1992; Middleton 1992; Nelson 1992).

The teacher's *lifestyle,* both in and outside school – his/her latent identities and cultures – impacts on views of teaching and on practice. Becker and Geer's (1971) work on latent identities and cultures provides a valuable theoretical basis. Lifestyle is, of course, often a characteristic element in certain cohorts: for instance, work on the generation of 1960s teachers would be of great value in studying professionals who came in with profound and particular commitments to education as a vehicle for social change and social justice. In a case study of a teacher, focusing on his lifestyle, Walker and I stated:

> The connections between youth culture and the curriculum reform movement of the sixties are more complex than we first thought. For Ron Fisher there definitely is a connection; he identifies strongly with youth culture and feels that to be important in his teaching. But despite his attraction to rock music and teenage life styles it is the school he has become committed to, almost against his own sense of direction. Involvement in innovation, for Ron at least, is not simply a question of technical involvement, but touches significant facets of his personal identity. This raises the question for the curriculum developer, what would a project look like if it explicitly set out to change the teachers rather than the curriculum? How would you design a project to appeal to the teacher-as-person rather than to the teacher-as-educator? What would be the effects and consequences of implementing such a design?
>
> (Goodson and Walker 1991: 145)

This, I think, shows how work in this area begins to force a reconceptualization of models of teacher development. We move, in short, from the teacher-as-practice to the teacher-as-person as our starting point for development.

The teachers' *life cycle* is an important aspect of professional life and development. This is a unique feature of teaching. For the teacher essentially confronts 'ageless' cohorts. This intensifies the importance of the life cycle for perceptions and practices.

Focus on the *life cycle* will generate insights into many of the unique elements of teaching. Indeed, so unique a characteristic would seem an obvious starting point for reflection about the teacher's world. Yet our research paradigms face so frankly in other directions that there has been little work to date in this area (see Huberman 1993).

Fortunately, work in other areas provides a very valuable framework. Some of Gail Sheehy's somewhat populist work in *Passages* (1976), *Pathfinders* (1981) and *New Passages* (1995) is, I think, important. So, also, is the research work carried out by Levinson (1979) on which some of Sheehy's publications are based. His work, while regrettably focused only on men, does provide some very generative insights into how our perspectives at particular stages in our life crucially affect our professional work. (For women's lives, see later work published by Levinson and Levinson 1996.)

Take, for instance, the case study of John Barnes, a university biologist. Levinson is writing about his 'dream' of himself as a front-rank, prize-winning biological researcher:

> Barnes's dream assumed greater urgency as he approached 40. He believed that most creative work in science is done before then. A

conversation with his father's lifelong friend around this time made a lasting impression on him. The older man confided that he had by now accepted his failure to become a 'legal star' and was content to be a competent and respected tax lawyer. He had decided that stardom is not synonymous with the good life; it was 'perfectly all right to be second best'. At the time, however, Barnes was not ready to scale down his own ambition. Instead, he decided to give up the chairmanship and devote himself fully to his research.

He stepped down from the chairmanship as he approached 41, and his project moved into its final phase. This was a crucial time for him, the culmination of years of striving. For several months, one distraction after another claimed his attention and heightened the suspense. He became the father of a little boy, and that same week was offered a prestigious chair at Yale. Flattered and excited, he felt that this was his 'last chance for a big offer'. But in the end Barnes said no. He found that he could not make a change at this stage of his work. Also, their ties to family and friends, and their love of place, were now of much greater importance to him and Ann. She said: 'The kudos almost got him, but now we are both glad we stayed'.

(Levinson 1979: 267)

This quotation, I think, shows how definitions of our professional location and of our career direction can only be arrived at by detailed understanding of people's lives. Studies of professional life and patterns of professional development must address these dimensions of the personal.

Likewise, *career stages* and *career decisions* can be analysed in their own right. Work on teachers' lives and careers is increasingly commanding attention in professional development workshops and courses. For instance, the Open University in England has used our book, *Teachers' Lives and Careers* (Ball and Goodson 1985), as one of its course set books. This is a small indication, yet symptomatic of important changes in the way that professional courses are being reorganized to allow concentration on the perspective of teachers' careers.

Besides the selection of career studies in *Teachers' Lives and Careers*, a range of new research is beginning to examine this neglected aspect of teachers' professional lives. The work of Sikes *et al.* (1985) and Goodson and Sikes (2001) has provided valuable new insights into how teachers construct and view their careers in teaching. More recent work on women's lifestyles, to add to earlier work on men's life stages, will help new studies in this area (see Levinson and Levinson 1996; Middleton 1997).

Moreover, work on teachers' careers points to the fact that there are *critical incidents* in teachers' lives, and specifically in their work, which may crucially affect perception and practice. Certainly, work undertaken on 'beginning teachers' has pointed to the importance of certain incidents in moulding teachers' styles and practices (see Lortie 1975).

Other work on critical incidents in teachers' lives can confront important themes contextualized within a full life perspective. David Tripp's (1994) work provides a range of elegant examples of critical incident studies. Also, Kathleen Casey has employed 'life history narratives' to understand the phenomenon of teacher dropout, specifically among female and activist teachers (Casey 1988, 1992; Casey and Apple 1989). Her work is extremely illuminating of this phenomenon, which is currently receiving a great deal of essentially uncritical attention given the problem of teacher shortages. Yet, few of the countries at the hard edge of teacher shortages have bothered to fund a serious study of teachers' lives, to examine and extend our understanding of the phenomenon of teacher dropouts. I would argue that only such an approach affords the possibility of extending our understanding, and this is particularly important when new initiatives, such as those suggested by the Labour Government in the UK, seek to bring back teachers who are over 50 into the profession.

Likewise, as with many other major themes in teachers' work, the question of teacher stress and burnout would, I believe, be best studied through life history perspectives. Similarly, the issue of effective teaching and the question of the take-up of innovations and new managerial initiatives. Above all, in the study of teachers' working conditions, this approach has a great deal to offer.

Studies of teachers' lives might allow us to see the individual in relation to the history of her or his time, allowing us to view the intersection of the life history with the history of society, thus illuminating the choices, contingencies and options open to the individual. 'Life histories' of schools, subjects and the teaching profession would provide vital contextual background in this respect. The initial focus on the teachers' lives, therefore, would reconceptualize our studies of schooling in quite basic ways (see Goodson 1991; Goodson and Sikes 2001).

While these foci for studying teachers' lives are by no means exhaustive, they do indicate how substantial the insights provided by such work might be. As we have seen, there are dangers in pursuing such work at a time of rapid restructuring, but to forego such work would be even more dangerous. Teacher perspectives on change are crucially important, and developing our longitudinal understanding of how teachers' practice is being transformed by contemporary changes is central to understanding the ongoing transformation of schooling. As the work in the next section evidences, just as important is realizing how teachers' personal beliefs and mission relate to new reform efforts. For, as will be seen, reforms that ignore these matters may be destined not to be high-profile successes but high-cost failures.

Part 2

six

Introduction: Studying educational change

The first section of the book advocates the use of life and work histories of teachers. This has been a major methodological device in most of the work that I have undertaken in the past decade.

The next three chapters are chosen to illustrate how immersion in detailed studies of teachers' life and work can further our contextual and theoretical understanding of broad movements of educational change. They show the transition from 'stories of action' to 'theories of context' which is a central objective of this kind of work.

In the last four years, I have been directing (along with Andy Hargreaves) a longitudinal study of change in schools funded by the Spencer Foundation, in New York State and Ontario, Canada. As we have developed our grounded historical theories of change, we have begun to grapple with the nature of the timing and conditions of change. We have also been focusing on the relationship of professional knowledge to educational change and, within this, the explanatory potential of studying teachers' life and work patterns within contexts of change and reform.

This has driven us to examine reform initiatives and restructuring in a new light and also to revisit the enormously important pioneering work of change theorists from the 1960s onwards, for example Huberman and Miles (1984); Fullan (1987, 1991, 1999); Fullan and Stiegelbauer (1991), and the like. What our studies evidence is the seismic shift in the conditions of change in the past few years. In the period since 1989, the triumphalist 'end of history' period of globalization, the velocity of change and the nature of change have dramatically altered.

From the 1960s to the 1980s, change theory rightly concentrated on what early change theorists called 'innovation' – changes largely generated by internal agents in the schools and broader educational administration. External agents were referred to in change theories of this time but still within the frame of educational systems.

In these times, change was conceptualized in stages which began with initiation and moved to implementation and continuation. The whole process took place as a result of educational agentry.

Change, then, is a linear process:

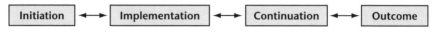

(Fullan and Stiegelbauer 1991: 48)

Our work, alongside a good deal of recent work, shows how substantially the conditions and velocity of change have been transformed in the past decade. Unless we change gears in our reform initiatives and associated change theories, we shall be left behind in the actually existing world of schooling. To put it brutally, we are faced with reforms, restructurings, changes and change theory that must move fast or else will be accused of being 'historically illiterate'. There are three issues that relate to historical illiteracy, if we accept the premise of a seismic shift in the last decade of the twentieth century.

First, in change theory there has been some talk about change as a process, an understanding encapsulated in Fullan and Parks's (1981: 49) insightful phrase that: 'change is a process, not an event'. But while this process notion has been recognized, there has been little serious longitudinal and socio-historical analysis of processes over time. Work is urgently needed, as with our Spencer project, on the socio-historical patterns of change, on change as a primarily socio-political process.

Secondly, the enormously valuable pioneering work of the Stanford Center, directed by Milbrey McClaughlin, encourages us to look more closely at the *contexts* of change. Hence, more work is urgently recommended on the times and spaces wherein change is promoted, nurtured, consolidated and continuing. Change is not an outcome in the postmodern world: it is a condition. The historical work of the French Annaliste School is of great value in analysing the historical 'conjunctures' of change. When change is a condition, much of the change is part of a global exhortation and expectation generated multinationally and then pursued at local and personal level. Thirdly, with change as a condition, the importance of personal passion and purpose is transformed. In modern times, the personal was subsumed in wider progress narratives. This marriage of the personal and political has now been annulled and new contracts are being negotiated. We find ourselves increasingly analysing how professional life and work in the form of personal missions and projects interlink with internally generated and externally mandated changes. It is this third dimension which I call the 'personality of change'.

A mass of work is now beginning to chip away at our understandings of the personal and emotional aspects of, and investments in, change: the work of Gardner (1993) on creative minds; of Goleman (1995) on emotional intelligence; of Hargreaves (1998) on the emotions of education; of Csikszentmihalyi's (1991) studies on life themes and 'flow'; of teachers' life and work (Goodson 1992); and teachers' stories (Middleton 1993; Munro 1998). All of these are symptoms of a growing awareness of the absences that sit at the heart of the predominantly technical and managerial paradigms of educational change and reform.

In the modernist periods, this absence was not of fatal significance since often personal and political projects interlinked and sometimes merged. With the postmodern collapse of public life, public space and public projects (Goodson 1999), this absence of the personal can sometimes cause a haemorrhage at the heart of change and reform missions.

Devoid of passion and purpose, many hugely funded reforms and changes are languishing, often producing results which are minimal or even contradictory. The neglect of the personal needs to be rapidly remedied, not least in the field of change theory. It is to be hoped that the re-embrace of the personal will humanize and galvanize the patterns of social change that we undertake in the future.

The definition of the 'personality of change' as a key issue comes not out of some abstract reconceptualization of change theory. The idea has been persistently raised by teachers on the Spencer Project. As an insight into the hidden workings of the project, let me explain how these issues came to the fore. As part of the project, we had been developing a structured interview on the teacher's life and work. We decided to add a final question which asked the teachers: 'Are there any interests and projects outside teaching that you would like to tell us about?' At this point in the interview, a significant section of teachers became animated in quite a new way. Their body language indicated that here, at last, was an issue that touched their personal passions and purposes in ways that teaching had ceased to do. It was as if here were some new 'boutique identity projects' which offered new possibilities for teachers that their work in schools could no longer provide.

For instance, one woman teacher told us excitedly how in the evenings she was training as an occupational therapist and would soon start her own business. Suddenly, there she was sitting on the edge of her seat full of excitement and purpose, whereas before she had been sitting lethargically recounting the way her job was being bureaucratized and deprofessionalized by the new state guidelines and patterns of governance. In the school, her sense of personal agentry and purpose was under attack. Her new project as an occupational therapist, working for herself, offered a chance to reclaim power and purpose, to reclaim an identity project, to reinvent a self.

Reflecting on these interviews, one could begin to see how so many of the reforms and changes which had aimed to redirect and reenergize teaching and learning might well have the diametrically opposite effect. It was as if teachers were taking their 'hearts and minds' away from teaching to other places where they might be cherished and utilized.

As the project developed, we began to dig deeper into these issues in some of the life history interviews that we conducted. The concern in these life history sessions (Goodson and Sikes 2001) was to develop a full sense of the teacher's life and work, but to embed that within wider understandings of the 'whole life' of the teacher; to see, in short, how teaching fitted into the complex mosaic which is a person's life.

The final chapters in this section look at the broader cycles of educational research intentions and patterns of teacher professionalism in the contemporary era of educational change and restructuring.

seven

The personality of change

In this chapter, a case study of one teacher is provided to show how the issue of the 'personality of change' emerges and develops in the work funded by the Spencer Foundation. This work has focused on eight schools: four of these schools are located in New York State in a downtown industrial area. The teacher in question has taught all of his professional life in downtown urban schools. From this case you will see how I have come to argue that 'it is important and appropriate to give personal change a prime place in the analysis of change' (Goodson 2001: 57).

In a later section, I show how personal missions are related to particular images and stages of professionalism, and in the final section I argue that the loss of teachers' 'hearts and minds', their 'passions and purposes', can lead to institutional memory loss in our schools – to an accelerating sense of forgetting whole patterns of professional behaviour. If pushed to extremes, this will leave teaching as technical delivery divorced from patterns of caring commitment, vocational purpose, and emotional ownership and investment.

The teacher that provides our exemplary portrayal works in an urban High School in New York State and specializes in English literature. He recounted how he came to be a teacher and, from the beginning in the interview, this teacher began to touch on the emotional and personal aspects of his teaching. Because he had not trained as a teacher, he judged that 'I was faking it for the most part for [the] first five years':

> But I realised early on that there were certain things that I did pretty
> well. I could build up a rapport with the class very quickly; I could get
> them interested in the literature very quickly. The lesson planning *per se*

was difficult for me, but I managed after a few years to develop my own little techniques and styles. But that's how, just in terms of background, that's how I got into it. I just sort of slid into teaching. I have to say my . . . one thing I've recognised after, because I have a great deal of interest in psychology . . . I've realised that I'm basically an introverted person . . . if I'd done it when I was in high school, I probably would have been introverted, intuitive, feeling, perceptive. But I've had to – for teaching purposes – develop another personality who is extroverted, intuitive, thinking, . . . the perception means I'm still teaching by the seat of my pants. I'm not the kind of person who can say, three months from now we'll be on page six. I've never been that and I've often resented those administrators and those decrees from on high that say that that's the only way you can teach.

But I have . . . I now have this sort of a personal life that is very introverted. When I go home . . . I have this space in the morning. I get here at 5:30 in the morning and the kids don't get here until 7:30 and I need that absolute quiet. That's when I grade papers, that's when I sort of plan things and so on. And then when I get home from school at the end of the day, I've got about two hours or three hours before my wife gets home and I just listen to music and basically decompress. And if I don't get those moments of solitude, I can't think. I have a great deal of respect for those teachers who, you know – they're involved in clubs. I've done clubs. I did the Olympics of the Mind; I've done the Masterminds, the Brainstormers, academic competition, that sort of thing. And I used to . . . there was a time when I would stay after school for an hour with kids, just chatted with them which I always welcomed, but I still need that decompression time. I think it's . . . I've worked into my schedule a way to sort of honour the part of me that's the basic root of me.

*[**Interviewer**] I want to touch in a way on something that you've said just a few moments ago. You talked about your need for space at the beginning and end of the day, so that's sort of a relation to your work at school. How would you describe how your work as a teacher affects your life outside of school? This is kind of going in the other direction.*

Yeah, that's probably even more important really because . . . and it's one of the problems I'm facing when I think about retirement because I have no idea. I do not . . . I cannot imagine . . . I mean I've lived in schools for 48 years, you know, what do people do? How do you do this? What is there? There's a rhythm, there is a structure, there's a set of gestures, and there's a stance that's part of the job that is in my fibre. Whenever I read, I cannot read without thinking, could I teach this, what's this teaching me about students, what's this teaching me about literature that I could give to my kids, is there a passage in here that I could lift? When I go to a movie, when I listen to music, everything . . . I'm thinking in terms of is this teachable, is this important, what's this tell me about the era that we live in and how is that reflected in my students' lives and so on. The more I think about it, the scarier it gets because if I didn't have that outlet, if I didn't have . . . and in many ways – and this is the introversion, I think – that in many ways teaching is for me a very selfish act. It is . . . as long as it's satisfying, as long as I'm getting a chance not just to, you know . . . I think students would tell you that I don't proselytise, I don't . . . I think most of them would say one of the strengths of my teaching method is that I listen. But that listening is not an act of kindness, it's an act of selfishness. I feed on ideas. I feed on points of view. I feed on little insights and little ideas and the stronger a class . . . if I can go away from a class period where we've discussed a work of literature and I say, 'My God, I never thought . . . I've taught that story 20 times; I never realised that before.' That's like something in my life, his life, her life, whatever and then I get charged. I get absolutely charged by that. And that is the most gratifying and selfish aspect, that the more selfless I become, the more selfish the interaction really is, the more satisfying it is. And I tell the kids, 'I'm like a car battery. I can run the lights for a while, but if the engine's not running, I'm going to die. If you guys don't feed something to me, I'll turn into just Joe Schmo teacher where I'm just sort of going through the motions and giving assignments.' But if you have one kid asks one question that gets me and a couple of other kids going, the battery can, you know, power . . . you know, it has incredible power.

So yeah, in terms of private life and public life, even though I keep them very separate at this sort of real level or the concrete level, I keep them separate. At the inner level, I can't separate them. I used to and it was because I got so much out of my kids. I used to spend a lot more time with young people and I still prefer the company of young people. I really don't . . . I don't seek out the company of adults. I don't have a lot of friends, especially adult friends. I prefer the company of minds that are still trying to figure things out rather than people who've figured them out. And that . . . you know, I'm a solitary person in that way. I used to have a lot of kids that would come around after school and it's . . . I hope it's not because of a change in me, I think it's because of a change in kids, that they're much less open to an intellectual relationship with an adult. It just doesn't happen as much here at this school. I'm sure it happens in some places, but it doesn't happen as much up here anymore.

These sections help us to come to know the teacher and his personal mission in a peculiarly intimate way. This is in fact a teacher who has won a wide array of prizes and awards for his exemplary work. Those of his students whom we have talked to all agreed on his massive commitment, not least to disadvantaged students, and his willingness to spend time outside school hours following up their interests with them. The commitment and vocation of this teacher is, in short, almost legendary within his school and community. Moreover, seeing himself as some kind of 'public intellectual', and being judged that way by many of his peers, his judgement of the new reforms and change initiatives is well worth listening to:

> . . . I think the way things have been structured downtown,[1] that business type mentality, the statistics based mandates, you know we're gonna get the scores, we're gonna raise this rather than . . . And I know it's sort of pie in the sky idealistic to say, you know, wouldn't it be nice if we talked about learning, if we talked about human beings and what kids turn into and lifetime learning. You know, wouldn't it be nice instead of 'at the end of this grade, they're gonna pass this test'. I know that's an idealistic expectation, but I think that unless somebody is . . . unless somebody talks that way, that mentality, that McDonaldisation of education is gonna become more firmly entrenched, that their power is going to become greater. That teachers are going to, first out of frustration, then out of who gets hired, become passive deliverers of pre-digested curriculum. Which is what they would like to see. They would like to eliminate personality and to go back to . . . you know the original question's about me. If nothing else, I'm just a human being in front of a bunch of other human beings giving a part of myself that I care about and giving them things that I care about. And the more we get away from that, I think the more we get away from real learning . . .

> I have two sayings about education that always confuse or anger people. One, most education takes place in the corner of the eye. It's not what we aim at that kids really learn and really makes a difference, it's those peripherals. The scholars and the educrats want to eliminate peripheral vision, but it's all about the corner of the eye. And the other thing is, and this sounds like an anarchist statement – maybe it is. Education is too important to leave to chance. And by that I mean real chance. The chance that any kind of good person . . . I guess that's not total chance . . . can get in front of kids and can be in and amongst kids. That if something is really going to happen, if something really comes from education, it's gonna be because kids have been exposed to multiple points of view, truly multiple points of view. Not pre-decided

---

[1] 'Downtown' is the location of the educational bureaucrats who run the city school system.

diversity, but real diversity of points of view, approach, and so on. You know what people want to do . . . what so many educrats want to do is find a kind of teaching, a kind of curriculum, a kind of teacher that they can replicate and put into a classroom. . . . I'd like a laid back teacher who just talks with the kids, I'd like somebody who's going step by step through a process. So the kids are not only learning content, they're learning ways of being in the world and thinking about the world through personalities. And educrats are scared out of their minds of personality, but that's what it's about. It's about their personalities, our personality, it's about interactions . . . And change is not going to take place until they find a way to . . . they find a language and they find a space for talking about human personality and how people relate.

This plea from a prize-winning teacher strikes me as symptomatic of the dilemma of many caring professionals in the world of globalized corporate rule making. In his new book, *The Corrosion of Character*, Richard Sennett (1999) poses the problem in a similar way. He starts by focusing on Rico, the college-educated son of the janitor, Enrico, whom he case-studied in the book *The Hidden Injuries of Class* (Sennett and Cobb 1972). Sennett shows how Rico lives in a world where the corporation encourages weak commitment and low trust:

> Institutional loyalty is a trap . . . Detachment and superficial cooperativeness are better armour for dealing with current realities than behaviour based on values of loyalty and service.
>
> (Sennett 1999: 25)

Sennett shows the problem this poses for life in the family, but we might see the same analogical problem in transposing this to caring professionals in the school, 'transposed to the family realm, "no long term" means keep moving, don't commit yourself, and don't sacrifice' (Sennett 1999: 25).

The dilemma is put succinctly in this way:

> Behaviour which earns success or even just survival at work thus gives Rico little to offer in the way of a parental role model. In fact, for this modern couple, the problem is just the reverse: how can they protect family relations from succumbing to the short-term behaviour, the meeting mindset, and above all the weakness of loyalty and commitment which mark the modern workplace? In place of the chameleon values of the new economy, the family – as Rico sees it – should emphasise instead formal obligation, trustworthiness, commitment, and purpose. These are long-term virtues.
>
> (1999: 26)

In some ways, I believe the same dilemma is posed for caring professionals in the school – they see the erosion of trust, commitment and community in the new world of tests, accountability, new contracts and new management technologies. By bringing the world of business into the school, the same collapse of trust and loyalty is threatened. A very dangerous experiment in a world where goodwill, vocation, personal care and commitment are so central.

Sennett sees the contrast between corporate work and the family, posing a series of questions:

> How can long-term purposes be pursued in a short-term society? How can durable social relations be sustained? How can a human being develop a narrative of identity and life history in a society composed of episodes and fragments?
>
> (1999: 26)

He concludes:

> The conditions of the new economy feed instead on experience which drifts in time, from place to place, from job to job. If I could state Rico's dilemma more largely, short-term capitalism threatens to corrode his character which bind human beings to one another and furnishes each with a sense of sustainable self.
>
> (1999: 26–7)

I believe this dilemma – as our data show – is evident in the caring professional's experience of the school. The new reforms threaten to corrode the character of our teachers and, therefore, our schools. If this process continues, there will truly be few places left from which to build again a sense of renewable commitment and trust. I think, as educationalists, we should stop presenting educational change as a neutral process that we help facilitate in the name of progress and improvement. We need to turn urgently to questions not about the 'technicality of change' but about 'the personality' and, indeed, 'morality of change'.

In the case study of a teacher presented in this text, the details of this teacher's working life and his judgements about reform and change are provided to ground the argument about the 'personality of change'. The complexity of teachers' professionalism is clearly evidenced in this testimony, as is the denial and essential deafness to this complexity that can be found at the heart of so many recent reform and restructuring initiatives. What his testimony shows is that teacher professionalism is complex and not definitive: there is no absolute model. Each teacher has to construct a personal professionalism that suits his or her life history, training, context and, above all, personality. A great deal of that professionalism is learnt, constructed and necessarily sustained in the everyday working environment of the school. Teacher professionalism and commitment is like a delicate natural ecology, and the role of reforms and change should be to construct sustainable environments where such professionalism can continue to flourish. This will not happen where the 'personality of change' is ignored.

Change theory needs to see school reform as an aspect of personal development and, conversely, has to view personal change and development among teachers as *itself* school reform.

eight

Personal missions and professional development

Many current school reforms and change theories start from the assumption that since all is not well with the schools (true), reform and change can only help the situation (false). The assumption is held that the clear enunciation of objectives, backed by a battery of tests, accompanied by accountability strategies, and confirmed by a range of financial incentives and payments by results, will inevitably raise school standards. The teacher is positioned as a key part of this delivery system, but the technical aspects of teacher professionalism are stressed, rather than the *professional biography* – the personal missions and commitments that underpin the teacher's sense of vocationalism and caring professionalism.

We can overstress this growing technization element which is far from universal, and we can overstate the attack on the teacher's sense of vocation. Nonetheless, what is irrefutable is that there has been little work on the 'personality of change'. In very few instances have school reforms or change theories been promulgated which place personal development and change as central 'building blocks' in the process. Instead, changes have been pursued in ways that seem to insist this will happen, *in spite* of the teacher's personal beliefs and missions. All too often, the 'personality of change' has been seen as the 'stumbling block' of real reform, rather than as a crucial 'building block'.

In this section, I want to evidence why such a view is potentially catastrophic for the current wave of reforms and change initiatives. Before I do this, however, let us examine a common myth in current school restructuring. It has a number of different embodiments, but goes something like this: in the old days (the sixties and seventies), in many Western countries, we operated loosely organized democratic social services and welfare states.

Because the economies were affluent, discipline was fairly casual, and school teachers (like other professionals) were allowed uncommon degrees of autonomy and professional self-direction. The result was a weak sense of social discipline and low school standards.

Now those days are over, governments are now firmly in control of the schools – objectives and tests are being clearly defined, and school standards and discipline will steadily improve.

With regard to the teachers, the story goes this way. The old days of professionals as autonomous and self-directed are over: the 'new professional' is technically competent, complies with new guidelines and ordinances, and views teaching as a job where, like others, he/she is managed and directed and delivers what is asked. Educational change at the level of teaching means replacing, as soon as possible, the 'old professionals' with the 'new professionals'. Once this task is completed and the 'old professionals' have been 'mopped up', a new, more efficient and improved schooling system will emerge.

In some ways, this story is similar to the restructuring initiatives pursued in a range of industries and services, but I want to suggest that in education in particular it is proving a dangerous package to pursue. Let us look at this from the perspective of teachers. From the point of view of the 'old professionals', the pattern is clear: 'the game is up', they are told. Either they abandon their dreams of a professional autonomy or they take early retirement. The results have been predictable everywhere – a huge rush of 'early retirements', alongside a group of teachers who 'hang in' in a state of despair and disenchantment.

For the reformers, this might be deemed a small transitional price to pay for replacing the 'old professionals' with 'new delivery conscious professionals'. But there we must stop: is it really that simple? Even in business, restructuring has proved more complex and contradictory than expected. In schools, the business is messily human and personal. Here, despair and disenchantment lead directly to uninspired teaching and spoilt student life-chances.

Ignoring the 'personality of change' might prove highly dangerous.

Talking to teachers, you can see what happens to their commitments. Here a prize-winning teacher of the 'old professional' sort talks:

> I could probably break down my 30 years into little maybe five- to six-year blocks. The first few years, maybe five years, I floundered. I was trying to figure this out. There were some things I did very well and other times I was a total disaster. But in that time, I was accumulating stuff. So there was that touchy feely sort of floundering person. And then when I got my creative writing class in 1975 and then when I got my first honours class in '79. From '75 until probably '85 was a kind of

golden age where the kids I was getting and my own intellectual curiosity were at a peak. And I was living off energy that was coming from outside and from inside. And I was constantly just looking for new stuff, finding new material, building up new stuff, and testing things out. And it was a great time period.

About 1985/1986, I think, I entered a period of real competence where I felt like I was someone with tools that I could use well and at will. I was a . . . I became a much more rigorous teacher. I began assigning a term paper, a 15-page term paper where the students had to read five novels by a particular author, do biographical research, do critical research, create a thesis and argue that thesis. A very, very rigorous, tough assignment and I knew how to teach it and I knew how to get it out of the kids. And I was . . . I became an expert, I think, in that time period. I was living on . . . it was probably more fun to be in that middle period class. But I think in terms of what I actually was teaching or what the kids were actually learning and the skills they were acquiring, I think that third period was probably the best when I was most skilful and I was giving the most to the kids.

Then I'd say in the last few years when I got involved in TLI and just a number of things have changed: the new Regents exam started popping up; the administration began to have more particular demands on what I was supposed to be doing.

What the teacher has talked to me about at length is how the new guidelines and texts have, over time, almost completely destroyed his commitment and ideals. This is a personal disaster, but I want to suggest that such a perception among 'old professionals' is a much wider disaster for the complex ecology of schools. The term 'old professional' needs to be further elucidated. I do not mean this to imply a particular professional of a certain age and stage, rather it means a view of teaching where the professionalism is expressed and experienced as more than just a job, but as a caring vocationalism. At heart, it means viewing the work of teaching as comprising more than material reward and technical delivery, as a form of work overlaid with purpose, passion and meaning. This sounds too pious (for it is not always – not in all circumstances – as we all have bad days, bad periods; we do mundane materialist things, of course), but it means a kind of professionalism where 'vocation' is part of the package, where 'ideals' are held and pursued. 'Old professional', then, captures an aspiration that is felt by both old and new teachers – it refers to a kind of professionalism and it is called 'old' merely because it was once more common and easier to pursue than it is in current circumstances.

In schools, the attack on 'old professional' vocationalism becomes a problem for a number of reasons:

- memory loss;
- mentoring loss;
- teacher retention and recruitment.

Let me take these in turn:

Memory loss

I have become very interested in what happens when the more mature members of an industry or community are given early retirement or subjected to change and reform that they disagree with, as is the case in so many of our schools. Interestingly, a range of new studies in Britain is looking at what happened to another delicate service industry – the railways. Tim Strangleman, himself a railway signalman, has been doing a PhD. on the railway industry. He has been particularly interested in the occupational identity that railway workers have, and their skill and pride in 'running the railways' – a complex task with a wide range of skills and techniques learned on the job and passed on from worker to worker. The railways are being restructured and divided into separate, self-managing regional companies, each with their own budgets. The workers' skill and pride in their jobs has been a central ingredient in the old national service – a feature of old railway professionals, one might say. But now with the restructuring:

> Any residual pride in the job is wearing thin as new managers, with no railway background themselves, foster the notion that 'it's just another job, like shelling peas'.
>
> (Newnham 1997: 28)

This reflects a similar phrase used again and again by younger teachers in our studies, 'After all, teaching is only a job, like any other.' In his railway study, Strangleman also makes connections. For instance, he

> makes a surprising comparison with the banking industry, where the term 'corporate memory loss' has been coined to describe the process whereby layers of unquantifiable knowledge, acquired through years of experience, were swept aside during the Eighties by an over-confident managerial class with no sense of the past. In the banking context, such tacit knowledge – 'rule of thumb, finger-in-the-air stuff' – might be the difference between sound and unsound investment. On the railways, it might be the difference between life and death.
>
> (Newnham 1997: 28)

This was written in 1997. Since then, Britain has witnessed a number of horrendous railway accidents, culminating in the Hatfield crash which led to the whole railway system being almost shut down for weeks.

The closure of Railtrack and its effective renationalization has led to a series of reports and commentaries which begin to face the reality of what has happened. For example, Keith Harper talks about the fact that:

> during this period, many disenchanted senior railway staff started to leave Railtrack, to be replaced in key appointments by people with little knowledge of the industry.
>
> (Harper 2001: 10)

Likewise, Christopher Green, Chief Executive of Virgin Trains, has argued that 'the most important criticism of the railway is that it has lost "the art of delivery" '. He says that the industry had thrown away 'the Sergeant Major of the track', by which he means the 'dedicated railwayman who daily used to inspect a ten mile length of track and knew what was wrong'. These men have gradually left the industry disillusioned and forgotten. They have been replaced by 'clever technology', dismissed by Green as 'hardly out of university experimental stage which have thrown up projects without being thoroughly tested' (Green 2001: 28).

Strangely, however, the learning curve seems impossibly long for those civil servants responsible for this initiative. Sir Steve Robson is the former second permanent secretary at the Treasury, and while he was at the Treasury he worked on several privatizations including the railways, and on the private finance initiative. In his analysis of the problem, he shows absolutely no awareness that work and motivation and the 'personalities of change' are a central issue. Instead, he returns to the common diagnosis that this is primarily a problem of money and financial incentives. In his conclusion to a recent piece, he argued:

> What about Railtrack? Where should we go now? The basic issue is the same – management and incentives. Rail infrastructure needs to be run by top quality managers who are incentivised, and empowered to do a good job. The issue for all of us who wish to see this country have a good rail system is whether the structure which comes out of administration will attract such managers and give them the right incentives and authority.
>
> (Robson 2001: 28)

The myopic absurdity of this diagnosis is breathtaking in the light of what has happened to the railways. It is as if the workforce and its inherited and ongoing expertise are of no importance in the delivery of the railway services. Again they return to the problem of how to incentivize the elite. This elite has been superannuated and incentivized to the most absurd level, and the result has been a catastrophic failure of delivery. One wonders what kind of experiences will be required for the learning curve in certain sectors of government to move upwards.

Perhaps, then, in school reform, the purging of the 'old professionals' in the face of new change and reform might be a similarly catastrophic move. All too clearly, attention to these aspects of the 'personality of change' is worth much greater attention.

Mentoring loss

Each school is a carefully constructed community: if the elders in that community feel disenchanted and disvalued, this is a problem for the community of the school. It then becomes a problem for the successful delivery of the educational services the school provides – in short, a problem of school performance and educational standards.

Robert Bly (1991) has written about the problems for any community when the 'elders' of that community are disenchanted, disorientated and disregarded. This problem is particularly relevant when considering teachers. Let me give a specific example of what is lost when a whole cohort or section of teachers responds in this way. In our studies, we have witnessed a number of schools where the sense of drift, of anarchy, of a lack of direction is palpable. In one of the schools – an innovative, landmark school in Toronto, founded in the sixties – the ex-headmaster judged the problem to be exactly as with the railways.

The old cohort of founding professionals had become disenchanted by the new changes and reforms. As a result, they either took early retirement or remained at work in a disaffected, disengaged way. The problem this posed, according to the ex-headmaster, was that nobody therefore took on the mentoring of young teachers. They just arrived and went to work; it was just a job and they followed management instructions and state guidelines as best they could. As a result, the 'old professionals' (in this specific case, mainly the elders) kept their professional knowledge to themselves and the chain of professional transmission was broken – the 'layers of unquantifiable knowledge, acquired through years of experience' remained untransmitted to the new generation of teachers. The school then suffered 'corporate memory loss'.

The result, apparently, was a school without passion or purpose, without direction. People turned up to do a job like any other job without a sense of overriding vocation or ideals and, as soon as they could, went home to their other life where, presumably, their passion and purpose resided and revived.

Teacher retention and recruitment

In the first two sections we have seen how 'old professional' vocationalism has declined in teaching, either formally through early retirement or spiritually because a wider cohort of teachers has become detached and disillusioned. At one stage, reform advocates and change theorists thought this evacuation by 'old professionals' a sign of the success of their strategy. As a result, they argued, schools would be rejuvenated and filled with eager advocates of the new reforms.

This has proved both wildly optimistic and misguided. The problem of retention (or the non-problem in the eyes of reformers) has quickly shifted to the problem of recruitment. The second is seen as a problem, because even the wildest change advocates recognize that schools have to be staffed!

What research is showing is that in many ways the problems of retention and of recruitment are related and have the same root cause. It seems that many of the younger cohorts of would-be teachers are looking at the job and making similar judgements to their 'old professional' elders. The 'purging of the old' stands alongside the 'turning-off' of the young.

To sum up the reasons, it is because, in Bob Hewitt's felicitous phrase, 'initiative and resourcefulness are banned' in teaching now, and, in his farewell article, 'I quit', he says:

> To see schools these days as filled just with bureaucratic bullshit is to seriously miss the point, however. Education has traditionally been about freedom. But there is no freedom anymore. It's gone. Initiative and resourcefulness are banned. Every school has become a part of the gulag. How else could inspectors time the literacy hour with stopwatches, or a teacher be dismissed over a bit of missing paperwork?
>
> (Hewitt and Fitzsimons 2001: 3)

While some younger recruits accept this form of occupational identity, far more are judging that they will take their initiative and resourcefulness into occupations that value rather than denigrate these characteristics. For example, Carmel Fitzsimons has just qualified as a teacher, but sees no possibility of actually practising. In the article, 'I quit', she says:

> I don't think teachers are uncreative – but creativity is being crushed out of them by the grinding cogs of bureaucracy and filing.
>
> To give you a glimpse: for every lesson a teacher is supposed to prepare assessment sheets from the previous lesson; they must then reflect upon the issues the assessment throws up. Then they must prepare a lesson plan – based on long-term, medium-term and short-term objectives from the curriculum; and having delivered the lesson, they must write up an evaluation of how the lesson went and then individually assess the progression of each child's learning. This can mean five sheets of written paper per lesson for each of the five lessons a day. Add the individual record of each child, the reading records and the collection of money for the school trip and you start to wonder

whether there is any time left for getting your coat on before legging it across the playground.

(Hewitt and Fitzsimons 2001: 2)

Interestingly, the same kind of transition from 'old professionalism' to 'new professionalism' seems to be at work in nursing. In a recent study of NHS nurses, Kim Catcheside found that patterns of professionalism were transforming themselves:

Modern nurses are a health hazard, the old-fashioned TLC-trained ones have all retired or resigned and the new lot, badly trained and poorly motivated, could not care less and are as likely in their ignorance to kill as to cure.

(Arnold 2001: 12)

Alistair Ross and a team of researchers have been studying teacher recruitment and retention for the past three years. Their findings make salutary reading for the advocates of reform and change:

We asked those who were leaving for other careers what it was that they saw as attractive in their new work.

Three-fifths of all teachers taking up work outside the profession do not find that teaching allows them to be creative and resourceful. These factors used to be one of the key defining elements of the teaching profession: people joined the profession because it used to offer them autonomy, creativity and the ability to use one's initiative.

What has happened to the profession that has caused these teachers, at least, to become so disillusioned that they seek alternative careers? This question, to teachers, is rhetorical. The ways in which teaching has become managed, has become 'accountable' and has been subjected to control and direction, have contributed to demotivation.

(Ross 2001: 9)

They found also that the problems of recruitment and retention were not primarily economic as has so often been argued:

We have also found that for teachers leaving the profession, it isn't high alternative salaries that are attracting them out. Of our sample of teachers leaving for other careers, only 27 per cent would be earning more than they earned as teachers; 27 per cent said that they would earn the same as they had earned as in their previous teaching post; and 45 per cent were going to posts paying *less* than they had earned in their last teaching post. It is the change in the nature of teaching that is behind the crisis points we have described.

(Ross 2001: 9)

Conclusion

Behind the question of the 'personality of change' stands the complex issue of what constitutes professional knowledge and action; what characterizes teacher professionalism? In our book, *Teachers' Professional Lives* (Goodson and Hargreaves 1996), we defined five kinds of professionalism as classical, flexible, practical, extended and complex. We predicted that in the twenty-first century a complex, postmodern, professionalism would emerge, based on a range of characteristics, most notably 'the creation and recognition of high task *complexity*, with levels of status and reward appropriate to such complexity' (1996: 21). We argued that this would lead to a more personalized notion of professionalism emerging, based upon

> a self-directed search and struggle for *continuous learning* related to one's own expertise and standards of practice, rather than compliance with the enervating obligations of *endless change* demanded by others.
>
> (1996: 21)

Geoff Troman (1996) has examined the rise of what he calls the 'new professionals'. This group accepts the new political dispensation and hierarchies of the reform process, new governmental guidelines, and national objectives and curriculum. However, some members of the group have taken aspects of the 'old professionals' ' view of the world. The 'old professionals' believed in teachers' collective control of their work, in professional and personal autonomy. In some ways, the 'new professionals' have found some way to continue being semi-autonomous and, in this sense, are pioneering a new complex professionalism which may moderate the bad effects of over-zealous reform initiatives.

But Troman was studying schools in the UK from the 1980s, through to the 1990s, before the excesses of the reform process noted above began to bite. He argued:

> The strategy of resistance within accommodation is possible, at this time, only because spaces exist within the work of teaching and management–teacher relations.
>
> (Troman 1996: 485)

In fact, recent reforms in a number of countries have sought to close these spaces for semi-autonomous personal and professional action. In doing so, they are tightening the screw too much and threatening to turn teaching into a profession attractive only to the compliant and docile, and conversely unattractive to the creative and resourceful. By pushing too far, they threaten to turn our schools into places of uniformity and barrenness – hardly a site on which standards will rise and educational inspiration flourish.

One way to view these changes and reforms is through the clear signs that it is the most creative and resourceful of our teachers who are the most disenchanted with new prescriptions and guidelines. In a recent survey, teachers generally have listed 'government initiatives' as the major reason why they wish to leave teaching. It is instructive to view any profession or workforce not as a monolithic entity but as made up of a number of segments. Looking at the teaching profession, we might distinguish three segments:

- an elite or vanguard made up of the top 10 to 20 per cent;
- a mainstream 'backbone' group comprising 60 to 70 per cent; and
- a borderline group comprising 10 to 20 per cent.

The elite group are the most creative and motivated group and often help define, articulate and extend the 'mission of teaching' generally, and of a school in particular. Their commitment to change and reform is a basic prerequisite for successful implementation: their disenchantment and disengagement leave change and reform as a hollow rhetoric. This is not least because of their mentorship and leadership of the mainstream group of teachers. This group, comprising 60 to 70 per cent of honest, hardworking professionals, makes up the backbone of the teaching profession. The interplay of mentorship and leadership between the elite and the backbone is reciprocal and vital in motivating and defining the teaching workforce. It is also central in the maintenance of a sense of vocation and mission.

The third group in any profession is the 10 or 20 per cent who are minimally involved: for them it is 'just a job' and some border on the competence level. This group has been the focus of many of the reforms and accountability strategies articulated by Western governments recently, yet one senses that like the poor they are 'always with us'. By focusing the reforms on this group, little is actually changed with regard to the performance and motivation of the group. However, and paradoxically, the world is transformed for the elite and the backbone. By attacking the small substandard groups, which all professions contain, many of the reforms have encountered a colossal downside by demotivating the vanguard and the backbone. Frankly, to use business jargon, the balance sheet's costs and benefits are deeply unsatisfactory – the benefits are minimal and the costs are colossal. If it were a simple question of financial bottom lines and profits, action would be taken immediately: the reforms would be aborted and new, more motivating and sensitive initiatives undertaken. However, since in education it is a question of human judgement and political face, one senses a long war of attrition before sensible judgements are made. In the meantime, the system continues its downward spiral.

The signs of disaffection grow daily; not just problems of teacher recruitment, but problems of student disaffection and recruitment, and the number of students being educated at home rather than at school continues to rocket under the National Curriculum in England. Meanwhile, in more vital and entrepreneurial environments like Hong Kong, the government is moving away from a rigid syllabus-defined subject-centred curriculum to a loose facilitating framework of 'key learning areas'. Each school defines its own curriculum within that facilitating framework, and the teacher's personal and professional judgement is given greater provenance. Here, respect for the 'personality of change' is built in to encourage greater creativity and competitiveness.

Above all, the reforms return some personal and professional discretion to the teacher: to the 'layers of unquantifiable knowledge acquired through years of experience', which only a foolish management group sort to expunge in the schools (as in the railways). In the railways, the result of the over-zealous pursuit of reform was a death-dealing dysfunctional system. In the school, the effect on student life-chances will amount to the same thing.

nine

Social histories of educational change

Educational change proposals resemble political parties. They represent a 'coalition' of interests and projects brought together under a common name at a particular point in time. When these separate segments of projects and interests are harmoniously organized, the social movement behind the political party or the educational change gains direction and force (Touraine 1981; Morrow and Torres 1999).

This chapter defines a number of different segments in educational change processes – the internal, the external and the personal. Internal change agents work within school settings to initiate and promote change within an external framework of support and sponsorship; external change is mandated in top-down manner, as with the introduction of national curriculum guidelines or new state testing regimes; personal change refers to the personal beliefs and missions that individuals bring to the change process. As Sheehy (1981) has argued, the embrace of change only happens with an inner change in people's beliefs and plans.

The more these segments are integrated and harmonized, the more it is likely that the social movement underpinning educational change will gather force and momentum. At certain times, segments may be tightly interlinked and integrated. At other times, a greater degree of separation might be evident, but even in periods of separation these segments stand in close relationship to one another.

Most commonly, one of the segments achieves primacy in driving educational change in a particular historical period and dominates the 'coalition of change' for a time. In the 1960s and 1970s, internal change agentry was often dominant, followed by a period where more external interests have driven the change process. Now we may be entering a period where personal agency begins to gather force in a world where what Giddens (1991) calls 'personal life politics' are increasingly powerful.

Change processes and historical periods

In the period following the Second World War, the internal professional power of educators began a period of substantial growth. This internal agentry was facilitated by external forces – expansionist economic conditions and policies; concern about Sputnik and new technological initiatives; the desire to build a 'great society' in the United States, and the development of more welfare-oriented societies in Europe (Sarason 1998). The period of 'cold war' between political ideologies set capitalist business values against systems of Communist production. Egalitarian social policies were often pursued and public education systems were heavily promoted as vehicles of common purpose and social good. Business values and the private sector lived in mixed economies, where public sectors provided a good deal of the public services of national systems (Reynolds *et al.* 1987).

In this period, which lasted well into the 1970s, and even longer in a few countries (for example, Canada), educators were seen as having large amounts of professional autonomy. Much educational change was left to internal educational experts to initiate and define. In these historical circumstances of substantial professional autonomy, change theory looked for the sources of initiating and promoting change to the educator groups who were internal to the school systems (Sarason 1996a, 1996b).

Internal educational change (Change Phase 1: 1960s and 1970s)

In the 1970s, I developed a model of curriculum change that scrutinized the internal affairs of change which were set against the 'external relations' of change. For instance, I argued that secondary school subjects passed through four stages as changes were initiated (see Goodson 1995c: 193–4):

1 *'Invention'* or change *formulation* might come about from the ideas or activities of education groups, sometimes as a response to 'climates of opinion'; or from inventions in the outside world (indirect external change forces); or in response to new intellectual directions and disciplines; or new school student demands (more direct internal change forces). The conceptualization of stages in this change theory drew a good deal on Bucher and Strauss's work on how professions change. They had argued that new change formulations, ideas and inventions normally exist in

several places over a period of time, but that only a few of these change formulations get adopted (Bucher and Strauss 1976: 19).

2 *'Promotion'* or change *implementation* occurred in school curricula, where new subjects were taken up by educator groups and promoted 'where and when persons (became) interested in the new idea, not only as intellectual content, but also as a means of establishing a new intellectual identity and particularly a new occupational role' (Ben-David and Collins 1966: 461). The response of science and mathematics teachers to computer technology is typical. In this stage, promotion of change arises from people's perception of the possibilities of basic improvements in their occupational role and status.

3 *'Legislation'* or change *policy establishment* extends the scope and impact of change. While changes were most often formulated and initially implemented by internal educator groups, their establishment and financial underwriting required the support of external *constituencies* or *policies* (Meyer and Rowan 1978). Change legislation is associated with developing and maintaining such discourses or legitimating rhetorics which provide automatic support from external groups for the now appropriately labelled activity, whether it be 'science' or 'SAT scores'.

4 *'Mythologization'* or *permanent change* institutionalizes the change in question. Once external automatic support has been achieved for a change category, a fairly wide variety of activities can be undertaken. The limits of action under the new change policy are only those activities that threaten the legitimating rhetoric and, hence, constituency support. Within these limits, changes are achieved and develop mythological, or taken-for-granted status. Essentially, this process represents granting a licence with the full force of the law and the 'establishment' behind it.

This stage theory of change provides an example of internally generated change models that were representative of this historical period, where public service provision was left a good deal in the hands of professional groups and where teachers and educationalists played central roles in initiating and promoting educational change.

The external relations of change (Change Phase 2: 1980s and 1990s)

Until the 1970s, change theory focused most usually upon the internally generated changes that were formulated and promoted by educator groups. Changing patterns of globalization and state control since 1989, including increasingly direct involvement of government agencies and corporate bodies in educational matters, make it necessary to revisit assumptions about internally generated change and to analyse what patterns of educational change now prevail (Menter *et al.* 1997; Webb and Vulliamy 1999).

Internal change agents in Change Phase 2 now face a 'crisis of position-ality' (Goodson 1999), where the power or positional strength of internal change agents to develop their own internal and personal visions of change has been substantially pre-empted by external interest groups. Internal change agents now find themselves responding to changes, not initiating them. In this crisis of positionality, instead of being committed internal change agents (with personal visions and ideals in harmony with the changes being sought), people become conservative respondents to, and often opponents of, externally initiated change. In this phase, the commit-ted internal change agent has become the (often) reluctant change exponent of externally generated plans. In Phase 2, the personal and institutional drives and desires that underpin change initiatives have largely been taken from the internal change agents' hands. The results of these ruptures between external and internal forces may be an educa-tional change process that is riven with conflict and dysfunctionality on an epic scale.

In the light of these developments, it is clear that change theory must now develop a stronger sense of history. When change was the internally defined 'mission' of many educators and external relations were developed later, educational goodwill and a sense of passion and purpose (Hargreaves and Fullan 1998) could often be assumed – although sustaining and generalizing such change often proved patchy and partial (Fullan and Stiegelbauer 1991). While large-scale legislated reform (Fullan 2000) might ostensibly promise stronger generalizability or a wider reach in the implementation of change, it rarely accounts for how seemingly common reforms are refracted through each school context, through the varied micro-climates and micro-politics of schools and through teachers' varying and sometimes resistant personal beliefs and missions. Thus, where large-scale reforms fail to incorporate teachers' senses of passion and purpose, such changes will actually face major problems of sustainability and generalizability. External direction and definition of large-scale reform does not ensure internally implemented and sustained improvement.

Given these complexities, Andy Hargreaves and I have been working on a multi-site research project to analyse and historically compare the changing *conditions of change* in American and Canadian secondary schools over three decades. Our methodology has been both historical and ethnographic (see Goodson and Ball 1984; Hargreaves 1986, 1994; Goodson 1995c; Fink 2000). In the schools we are studying, we have developed a historical archive and oral history of the changes and reforms that have been attempted within the schools. We have begun to see how, in the past half-century, educational change has followed a series of long as well as short wave cycles, not unlike the economy (Kondratiev 1984). In these cycles, the powers of internal pro-fessional groups and external constituencies have oscillated quite markedly and, in doing so, affected the change forces and associated change theories that we analyse and define.

An example: 'Durant School'

Let me provide an example, developed with Martha Foote, from the Spencer study (Goodson and Foote 2001). According to archival and interview data, the idea of an alternative school in Bradford, a small industrial city in upper New York state, was conceived in the late 1960s by an internal group of district teachers, students and parents. These individuals had banded together in an attempt to develop alternative educational opportunities in the local public high schools, especially in response to a wave of school rioting and the subsequent efforts to clamp down on the student population. This group believed that the key to learning did not lie in more restrictive and punitive regulations in the traditional school setting. Instead, they advocated a greater student role in developing and maintaining a flexible educational programme that responded to individual student needs and encompassed the entire city landscape as a learning environment.

After a year of meetings, this internal group took its plan to the district. The Board of Education passed a resolution of authorization and in September 1971 the 'Durant School' opened. A junior high and an elementary school, each with its own non-traditional mission, also opened in the district, and plans and materials were exchanged among all three. The educational change forces at this time, therefore, had some of the features of a social movement, as ideas were shared and disseminated among like-minded schools, not only locally but also throughout the United States.

As the years passed, 'Durant School' had to negotiate periodically with external constituencies in order to secure legitimacy and ensure its survival. For example, to meet state requirements for registration and approval, the school had to comply with state law regarding physical education and health instruction. It also had to concede to the use of Carnegie course units as evidence of a legitimate academic programme. Another time, when the district dictated an increase in maths and science credits for graduation, the school was forced to tinker with its programme. Yet, despite these changes, the school's overall integrity remained intact. It was allowed enough autonomy by the district and the state to continue to offer a non-traditional learning experience to its students. As the first programme director wrote, in a memo to staff,

> We have always approached program assessment and redesign from the standpoint of our beliefs, doing things because we felt they were right

and not because everyone else was doing them. That has been the source of our strength and the basis of our success.

(12 May 1983)

More recently, though, the forces of change have begun to alter drastically towards the more externally driven pattern noted earlier. Now, the school primarily responds to change developed by external groups. The most immediate and pressing example of this switch can be seen in the school's response to the state's adoption of five standardized exams, the passage of which will be mandatory for graduation. These exams are the manifestation of the push for 'higher standards', a push often spearheaded by the business sector and championed by the state commissioner of education. Though working tirelessly to secure a discretion (known as 'variance') in relation to the exams, the school has had to alter its curriculum and programme to accommodate these external changes. Teachers are now forced to teach classes specifically geared to the content of these state exams, instead of classes that they believe are educationally sound. Students can no longer develop programmes of study to meet their own individual needs, as they must enrol in these test-driven classes. The school, founded as an alternative to the regulations of the traditional high school, is now a victim of these very dictums (McNeil 2000). As one teacher stated in an interview,

> So the [state tests] are coming and I think it's a damn shame that that sense of autonomy, that ability to create your curriculum with high standards has to be thrown out every place by something that I think is artificial. It takes out the creativity of teaching and you're teaching to the test. Just the thought that I'm doing this is totally counter to what I believe, it really is, but you know, I'm a captive . . . You're selling your soul to the devil.

(October 1999)

The school is now challenged by the new mandate pushed by the state education commissioners to have students sit the state examination. This will transform the context and control of the school's curriculum and, in doing so, change the teaching/learning milieu. In this new change dispensation, change is externally mandated and only then internally negotiated.

Given these altered conditions of change, a combination of historical and ethnographic methods allows us to develop a more contextually sensitive change theory. This emerging theory arbitrates between the changing balance of external relations and internal affairs in different historical circumstances. In the current situation, our reformulated change model begins to take the following form:

1 *Change formulation.* Educational changes are discussed in a variety of external arenas including business groups, associated think-tanks, new

pressure groups like 'standards mean business', and a variety of relatively newly formed parental groups. Often these changes resemble world movements that can be traced back to the World Bank and the International Monetary Fund (Torres 2000). Much of the change is driven by a belief in marketization of education and the delivery of educational services to parental 'consumers' who are free to choose and to bargain over their provision (Kenway 1993; Whitty 1997; Robertson 1998).

2 *Change promotion* is handled in a similar fashion by external groups with varied internal involvement. As Reid has written:

> External forces and structures emerge, not merely as sources of ideas, promptings, inducements and constraints, but as definers and carriers of the categories of content, role and activity to which the practice of schools must approximate in order to attract support and legitimisation.
>
> (Reid 1984: 68)

3 *Change legislation* provides the legal inducement for schools to follow externally mandated changes. In some countries, schools are evaluated by examination results (which are published in league tables). Measures also exist or are underway to link teachers' pay to teachers' performance in terms of students' examination or test results (Menter *et al.* 1997). Such legislation leads to a new regime of schooling, but allows teachers to make some of their own responses in terms of pedagogy and professionalism. Overall, school change policy and curricula and assessment policy is thereby legislated, but some areas of professional autonomy and associated arenas for change can still be carved out. In certain countries (for example, Scandinavia), this is leading to progressive decentralization and a push for new professional autonomy. Again, the world movements for change are historically refracted by national systems.

4 *Change establishment.* While external change has been established systematically and legally, the power resides mostly in the new *categorical* understandings of how schools operate – *delivering* mandated curriculum, being assessed and inspected, responding to choice and consumer demands (Hargreaves *et al.* 2001). Much of the marketization of schools is taken for granted now in many countries and, in that sense, has achieved mythological status.

New educational change forces, then, are primarily driven by external constituencies and have followed the seismic shifts of the last decade in promoting marketization and globalization. But this is only the beginning of the story. As we noted earlier, schools are major repositories of social memory and their procedures, practices and senses of professionalism are historically embedded. New external changes, therefore, confront various kinds of 'contextual inertia' or 'social refraction' in schools themselves. Any change that is sustained will, therefore, result from the convergence of new change forces with the historical context of schooling. To analyse *sustainability of change*, we have to understand the *conditions of change*, and to do this we have to develop our historical and ethnographic studies. We cannot pursue the idea of *sustainability of change* without such understandings.

Without sensitivity to context, the new change forces may be shipwrecked in the collision with the hard sedimentary rocks of existing school contexts. Externally mandated change forces are all very well as a triumphalist symbolic action pronouncing the new world order, but unless they develop sensitivity to school context and to teachers' personal missions, the triumph may be short-lived and unsustainable, or we will see the emergence of a new purpose and function for teaching and schooling far removed from mandated intentions.

New disruptions in educational change (Change Phase 3: The new millennium)

The chain of change in the postwar period was fairly clearly enunciated and transparent. Internal missions of change were given primacy in the period of initiation and promotion. As MacDonald (1991: 11) has noted, 'We, the innovators, began under benign and supportive government and saw the problem largely as a technical one, under professional control.'

With liberal social democratic governments promoting inclusionary policy, the chain of change from internal affairs to external relations was often one of compatibility or harmonization. However, the West's triumphalism following the collapse of Communism in 1989 has ruptured this chain of change, presenting internal agents with a crisis of positionality. Their existing missions of change have been subverted and inverted by a range of externally generated and imposed missions of change, over which they have little influence and in which they have little investment or ownership. Far from being the favoured posture of the progressive educator, change has often become an unwelcome and alien imposition.

As the triumphalist period comes to an end, more thoughtful external change agents are beginning to renegotiate the balance of internal and external forces. What these agents and their associated educational advisers realize is that the move to externally driven change has gone too far, creating a danger of 'throwing the baby out with the bathwater'. The frustration that external constituencies have felt with the power of internal agents to pursue their own micro-political and personal missions has led to an all-out attack on these missions (Jeffrey and Woods 1996). As a result, the agents in schools who are actually charged with delivering change feel disempowered and under attack. When school-level change agents are so substantially demotivated, no wonder so many reforms are in trouble. Our Spencer research has unearthed a massive body of teachers, specifically preparing students for the state exams, who are being charged with delivering reforms in relation to which they feel uncommitted, disvalued and demotivated. Here are just a few examples from a huge file of reports covering all the schools we have been studying:

> As a profession, more and more freedom in the latitude of what and how I teach is slowly being eroded and transferred to administrative decision-makers (with no experience).

> It is an affront to my philosophy that professionals can make blanket statements about standards for all students when, clearly, entire groups of students are not having their needs met.

> The district has asked that we prepare our students for the new state exam. Such work is tedious, uninteresting, and time consuming for both the students and me. The paper load is overwhelming. It is also disruptive to the contents and sequencing of the curriculum. Students see prepping for the exam as a disconnected almost absurd activity . . . As a result of these frustrations, I've sunk into a period of depression . . . This year the nuts and bolts of curriculum, paper grading, and monitoring of students has left me no time or energy for the more global kind of thinking that charges my battery.

> Forcing these kids to endure state-mandated higher level science courses they can never pass is a crime . . . In my opinion, (the) state has lost its way in education. The state education board is so interested in reacting to media critics that they have ignored the needs of the children as they are supposed to be getting ready for adulthood.

> These changes leave me with more time for life outside the school. I'm putting less time into my work. Partly this is due to my skills. Teaching to the test is vastly easier than teaching what is needed for individuals, and takes less time, especially for someone who has done it for 20 years as I have. Unfortunately, I'm also putting in less time because of decreasing morale. I sometimes fall into a 'what's the use' frame of mind.

What these teachers are saying is that administrators and politicians are pushing inappropriate and politically motivated reforms, and that new testing regimes disvalue many students and attack teachers' sense of themselves as caring professionals, even if their work is paradoxically made technically easier.

The personality of change

New models of educational change need to reinstate the balance between the internal affairs, the external relations and the personal perspectives of change. The capacity of internal agents to *refract* externally mandated change is substantial and, with low staff morale and low staff investment, change can remain more symbolic than substantive (Popkewitz *et al.* 1982). If educational change is to move from the realm of triumphalist symbolic action into the realm of substantive changes in practice and performance, a new balance between personal, internal and external change will have to be negotiated. Only then will the issues of sustainability and generalizability be fully engaged with and change forces really move forward. Instead of forced changes, we will then have change forces as the new conditions of change engage collaboratively with the existing contexts of school life.

It is no longer sensible to limit the work on educational change to internalistic or even externalized models of institutional change. The enduring flaw in both these models has always been the degree of disconnection to individuals' personal projects. In postmodern times, with the salience of individual identity projects, this enduring problem is much exacerbated. When teachers detach their identity projects, their 'hearts and minds' from school, change is unlikely to be successful.

Traditional change theory either ignores people's personal investments in, or relationships to change; or, more subtly, it interprets people's personal projects in ways that make them organizationally manageable – viewing institutional concerns and individual concerns as being one and the same. For example, Hall and Hord's (1987) classic work, *Change in Schools, Facilitating the Process*, includes a concern with the personal domain of people's self-projects, but contains this domain within a concern about institutional innovation. They list the following 'stages of concern' about innovation:

Informational: A general awareness of the innovation and interest in learning more detail about it is indicated. The person seems to be unworried about himself/herself in relation to the innovation. He/she is interested in substantive aspects of the innovation in a selfless manner such as general characteristics, effects, and requirements for use.

Personal: The individual is uncertain about the demands of the innovation, his/her inadequacy to meet those demands, and his/her role in relation to the reward structure of the organization, decision making, and consideration of potential conflicts with existing structures or personal commitment. Financial or status implications of the programme for self and colleagues may also be reflected.

Management: Attention is focused on the processes and tasks of using the innovation and the best use of information and resources.

Issues related to efficiency, organizing, managing, scheduling, and time demands are utmost.

Consequence: Attention focuses on impact of the innovation on the student in his/her immediate sphere of influence. The focus is on relevance of the innovation for students, evaluation of student outcomes, including performance and competencies, and changes needed to increase student outcomes.

Collaboration: The focus is on coordination and cooperation with others regarding use of the innovation.

Refocusing: The focus is on exploration of more universal benefits from the innovation, including the possibility of major changes or replacement with a more powerful alternative. The individual has definite ideas about alternatives to the proposed or existing form of the innovation.

(Hall and Hord 1987: 60, fig. 2)

This influential work reveals its outdatedness by subordinating and subsuming personal projects of change within institutional ones. This perennially questionable position is particularly problematic given the conditions of postmodernity. While institutions do endure, everyday life and life politics also persist in other frames aside from them. Increasingly, individuals live outside institutional and traditional patternings; they are at once more free, yet more bereft. People's personal missions of change have to be understood within this new frame of the quest for personal meaning. To remake the connection between the institutional and the personal, we need to grasp each person's life theme or his/her story of purpose. Senge says this about stories of purpose as they emerge in interviews with a range of leaders in industry:

The leader's purpose story is both personal and universal. It defines her or his life's work. It ennobles his efforts, yet leaves an abiding humility that keeps him from taking his own successes and failures too seriously. It brings a unique depth of meaning to his vision, a larger landscape upon which his personal dreams and goals stand out as landmarks on a longer journey. But what is most important, this story is central to his *ability to lead*. It places his organisation's purpose, its reason for being within a context of 'where we've come from and where we're headed', where the 'we' goes beyond the organisation itself to humankind more broadly. In this sense, they naturally see their organisation as a vehicle for bringing learning and change into society. This is the power of the purpose story – it provides a single integrating set of ideas that gives meaning to all aspects of a leader's work.

(Senge 1995: 346)

This centrality of inner/personal concerns has been evidenced repeatedly in studies of institutional life. In her study of innovative individuals, Sheehy (1981: 101) has argued that with an outer change of situation, a transformation of work or institutional circumstances, 'the process always began with an *inner change* in their basic approach'. Change, then, most often begins with a transformation of people's personal perceptions and projects and flows outwards into the social and institutional domain.

Hence it is important and appropriate to give personal change a prime place in the analysis of change. This stands more institutionally driven theories of change on their heads. While these theories look at how to get people to change in institutions, the focus should instead be on how people change internally and on how that personal change then plays out, as and through institutional change.

The chain of change in personal matters follows a common sequence:

PHASES OF THE CREATIVE PROCESS	PHASES OF A SUCCESSFUL PASSAGE
Preparation *Gathering impressions and images*	**Anticipation** *Imagining oneself in the next stage of life*
Incubation *Letting go of certainties*	**Separation and incubation** *Letting go of an outlived identity*
Immersion and illumination *Creative intervention – risk*	**Expansion** *Deliberate intervention in the life conflict – risk*
Revision *Conscious structuring and editing of creative material*	**Incorporation** *Reflection on and integration of one's new aspects*
Dormancy – a creative pause for the replenishment of self	*Dormancy – for rest, reward, and play to offset stress of change*

(Sheehy 1981: 100)

Sheehy's work shows how each person is subject to ongoing change and renegotiation in the manner in which they organize their lives. If people are to bring the crucial dimensions of passion and purpose into their institutional projects, then these institutional missions have to reach out and connect with personal missions and emotions. In schools, the teacher's role is so central that change theories and projects which ignore the personal domain are bound to end up wide of their target.

From history to the future: new chains of change

It should now be clear that change models are required which systematically seek to integrate internal, external and personal sectors in new chains of change. This section tentatively defines a model of change theory and practice that could explore such areas of integration:

Mission	$\longrightarrow$	Institutionalize
Micro-politics	$\longrightarrow$	Institutionalized practices
Memory work	$\longrightarrow$	Communitize
Movement	$\longrightarrow$	Generalize

1 *Mission: institutionalize*
   In the new era, a mission of change will be defined and renegotiated by internal and external agents. While respecting external change forces, this mission will, from the beginning, accept that the delivery of change is centrally located in the hands of internal school agents and closely linked to their personal projects and concerns. To succeed, change must be part of their mission. Without internal investment and ownership, change will be both gruelling and grudging: not a prescription for sustainability or generalizability. Institutionalization depends on an accepted internal and personal mission, characterized by passion, purpose, investment and 'ownership'.

2 *Micro-politics: institutionalized practices*
   In negotiating internal missions, the micro-politics of change are central. Change missions have to be embedded in new institutionalized practices. This is the core of the new chains of change. The teachers' work, their professional labour, their personal concerns and instruments are at the heart of education. To change education is to change the teachers' work and vice versa. The delicate micro-politics of negotiating new professional practices cannot be delivered solely by external mandate and inspection. There must be internal renegotiation. Such renegotiation must be handled in painstaking internal micro-politics. Each school has its own instinctive micro-politics, just as each school has its own ecology. To trample in the 'secret garden' of the school is a very dangerous process, best left to those who know its ecology. The issue is how to ensure institutionalized practices are defined and accepted which follow new change missions.

3 *Memory work: communitize*
   A good deal of the negotiation of change involves confronting existing memories of schools and school practices. These memories of what constitute 'school', 'subjects', or 'teaching' do not just reside in internal agents' minds, but are also crucially and historically embedded in the wider community. Perhaps the most neglected aspect of change theory is the

need to develop community awareness of new reforms. In the postwar period, the coalition of professionals and government often preceded without due cognizance of local community opinion or the new change dispensation. The community will need to be involved in the definition and negotiation of reform initiatives.

4 *Movement: generalize*
Chains of change are perhaps viewed as small-scale social movements. New missions are defined, practices are initiated, supporters are mobilized and, finally, coalitions are formed. In past periods, progressive schools have often formed coalitions of other like-minded schools (Lieberman and Grolnick 1998). Acknowledgement of the social movement characterization of change forces would develop the capacity to sustain and generalize change missions across the internal, external and personal sectors.

Conclusion

Developing social histories of educational change, and to some extent also of change theory, alerts us to certain dangers as the 'conditions of change' themselves change. In Phase 1, internal missions were given priority, with mixed results and patchy generalizability in terms of the changes that were pursued. In frustration at this partial result, the pendulum of change initiatives and theory swung in Phase 2 towards externally mandated reform. Change was mandated and legislated by external constituencies. The result has been widespread demotivation and detachment of internal and personal missions.

A new phase of change now beckons, which acknowledges the force of personal identity projects under postmodernity and which seeks new integration with internal missions. Unless this new balance is achieved, change forces will be neither humanized nor galvanized. 'Change' will stand as a form of political symbolic action without personal or internal commitment or ownership.

Change and reform must be seen as going both ways in relation to school and context, both into and out from the school. This movement *both ways* is reflected in the importance of teachers' personal beliefs and internal missions. Educational change works most successfully when reform sees these personal commitments of teachers as both an inspiration for reform (which works best when carried by teachers as part of their personal–professional projects), and a necessary object of reform (the need to provide support for teachers to the point where they wish to take 'ownership' of the reform).

These crucial insights into the salience of teacher commitment explain the growing interest in teachers' professional lives (Goodson and Hargreaves 1996). As McClaughlin and Yee (1988: 40–1) have noted in US schools:

'The vitality of educational reform hinges to a significant degree on the extent to which teachers have a rewarding career. In education, where teachers comprise the technology, the link between individual responses to challenge and change and organisational effectiveness is direct and irreducible.'

The teacher's career, then, reflects these issues of commitment and personal satisfaction. These ingredients are not likely if change initiatives and theory ignore the personal projects and internal school projects so dear to teachers. These are the places to begin when building coalitions of change and change theory, above all, needs to start there once again. To paraphrase former President Bill Clinton, 'It's the teacher, stupid.'

ten

The educational researcher as a public intellectual

The multifaceted appeal of Lawrence Stenhouse, both to contemporaries and to new generations, is testified to in the wide range of lectures and testimonies which have sought to represent and characterize his work. For me, the central element in his appeal was that, in both his writing and his action, he spoke as a public intellectual; as one who expected his ideas to form the basis of influence and action in the public sphere. Moreover, his central concern was with education for empowerment and social justice. In an early draft manifesto for the Centre for Applied Research in Education, he stressed its role as a 'public service'. As we shall see, in some senses, the times in which he lived brought aid and sustenance to this view of an educational researcher's social and political purpose, but we should also be aware that he also existed in vigorously contested terrains. Towards the end of his life, he must have begun to glimpse the 'dark night' into which much of his vernacular humanism would be cast in the new order where there was to be 'no such thing as society'.

Public knowledge and public education have historically been subject to recurrent pendulum swings between the emancipatory/enlightenment vision and the darker forces of subordination and social control. From the point of view of public intellectual life, Thomas Paine expressed the high optimism of the Enlightenment when he argued, 'I am a farmer of thoughts and all the crops I raise I give away.' Well, we know what the free marketeers would think of that kind of high-mindedness, when only things that are done for profit are pursued or praised. But, in truth, public knowledge and public education have often been subjected to the kind of 'dark night' we have recently been experiencing.

In 1807, the British Parliament debated a bill to provide two years of free schooling for children aged 7 to 14 who could not pay fees. The Archbishop of Canterbury said it would subvert the first principles of education in his country that had been and, he trusted, would continue to be under the control of the establishment. One MP, Davies Giddy, is recorded in the 13 July 1807 edition of Hansard as having uttered the following prophetic words:

> However specious in theory the project might be of giving education to the labouring classes of the poor, it would be prejudicial to their morals and happiness; it would teach them to despise their lot in life, instead of making them good servants in agriculture and other laborious employment. Instead of teaching them subordination, it would render them fractious and refractory, as was evident in the manufacturing counties; it would enable them to read seditious pamphlets, vicious books and publications against Christianity; it would render them insolent to their superiors; and in a few years, the legislature would find it necessary to direct the strong arm of power toward them.
>
> (Giddy 1807: 798)

Interestingly, Noam Chomsky invoked the early 1800s as the last time when the rich and powerful and industrial interests had truly unlimited powers. Until now, that is. In his Cambridge lecture, he said (and he is speaking about current times):

> There has been a recognition on the part of very powerful sectors that they have the population by the throat. They have an opportunity not just to fight a holding action against the increase of human rights and labour rights and democracy, but actually to roll it back and to restore the utopia of the masters of the kind that was dreamed of in the 1820s.
>
> (Chomsky 1995: 17)

David Marquand, in a slightly more diplomatic manner, has described the characteristics of the last period in British life:

> The most obvious hallmark of the Thatcher and Major governments has been a ferocious onslaught on institutional autonomy, diversity and stability in the name of the rationality of the marketplace. Almost all the institutions which used to shield an unusually stable and diverse civil society from the arrogance of the politicians in temporary command of the state, or which embodied values and practices at variance with those of market economies, have felt the lash of this Tory Jacobinism . . . One result is that the core executive at the heart of this state – the tiny group of senior ministers and top officials who make up

the elective dictatorship which governs Britain – has to reckon with fewer countervailing powers than ever before in peacetime.

(Marquand 1994: 26)

Now the notion that the pendulum swings with regard to public knowledge is itself an ideological position, for there are certainly those, at the moment, who argue for the 'end of history' and, indeed, Chomsky himself has come close to this view. While the 'end of history' is plainly an absurd notion taken literally, it does question whether the current reallocation of global power constitutes a culminatory phase in the long march of the rich and powerful. If this were so, the assumption that the pendulum will one day swing back to more emancipatory notions of education has at least to be questioned if not, as yet, finally dismissed. If the 'end of history' fails to capture the nuances, certainly the end of hope – of particular hopes, such as social justice or redistribution – comes close to the mark. For the moment, as you will see, my position echoes the character in *Boys from the Blackstuff*, who, at the end of his life, still said 'I just can't believe there's no hope' (Bleasdale and Self 1985).

The reasons for starting with this rather broad canvas of commentary is that issues affecting educational research (whether as public intellectual work or not) are clearly affected by the current changes in the global economy. As education and schooling are themselves repositioned and restratified in the new global work order, so, inevitably, research on education is itself repositioned. In such a situation, even if people go on researching as they researched before, their work may have been repositioned: sometimes so as to shift substantially or even invert the relevance and effect of that work. The recent changes in the global economy, then, work at a number of levels: at levels of economic production, there is a much analysed *crisis of modernisation* and a consequent need to explore and interrogate the condition of postmodernity; but at levels of cultural production, it is to the aforementioned *crisis of positionality* that we should be turning. A crisis of positionality arises at this point, because high modern capital has successfully reconstituted and repositioned the social relations of production: the newly deregulated global circulation of capital substantially confines and repositions those social movements that have sought to tackle issues of redistribution and inequality. Welfare states, national trade unions, progressive movements and so on can be redefined by a press of the button which moves capital from 'intransient' national and local sites (economically inefficient sites) to more malleable sites (economically competitive sites). Global capital then has twin triumphs to celebrate: the emasculation of social democratic/egalitarian movements within the Western world, and the culminating destruction of alternative systems of production and distribution in the communist world. These twin triumphs leave would-be public intellectuals in a precarious and rudderless position; detached from past histories of action for social justice and divorced from hard-won visions of alternative futures. In the crisis of positionality there is no firm ground to stand on, and to remain in the same place is to risk one's position being changed nonetheless.

Locating the public intellectual

In locating Lawrence Stenhouse's role as public intellectual and in scrutinizing the changing terrain of the last thirty or so years, it is, I think, particularly instructive to examine the trajectory of the Centre for Applied Research in Education. The Centre was founded in 1970 by Stenhouse, but grew out of the Humanities Curriculum Project (HCP) which had begun in 1967.

HCP drew deeply on the egalitarian commitments of sections of postwar British society. The 'we're all in it together' spirit of the war emanated in the attempts to build New Jerusalem under the Labour governments of 1945–51. While watered down by subsequent governments, these social justice sentiments were still alive and well in the mid-1960s when HCP was conceived. The spirit is well captured in one of the first Schools Council working papers on raising the school leaving age:

> The problem is to give every man some access to a complex cultural inheritance, some hold on his personal life and on his relationships with the various communities to which he belongs, some extension of his understanding of, and sensitivity towards, other human beings. The aim is to forward understanding, discrimination and judgement in the human field – it will involve reliable factual knowledge, where this is appropriate, direct experience, imaginative experience, some appreciation of the dilemmas of the human condition, of the rough-hewn nature of many of our institutions and some rational thought about them.
>
> (Schools Council 1965, para. 60)

That such sentiments could be expressed by establishment figures in 1960s Britain shows that some powerful groups in society were committed to continuing egalitarian projects. It should be remembered that, at almost the same time in the USA, Lyndon Johnson was launching his 'Great Society' initiative. So far from building an egalitarian fortress, Britain was, in fact, part of a broader world movement. Noel Annan (1995) has written in his book, *Our Age*, of the substantial support within the liberal elements of the British establishment for social justice. He judges 'our age' lasted from 1945 until well into the 1970s.

One of the offshoots of the social justice movement was the curriculum development movement in schools – seeking to broaden educational opportunities for *all* pupils. As MacDonald recalls:

> In England, it was largely the lower reaches of the education system that constituted the recruiting grounds of innovation – the colleges of teacher training and the schools themselves. For these upwardly mobile but academically under qualified recruits, there was no ready-made entry into the discipline-based heights of the institutional order. The universities had not been party to the political settlement that saw the ministry, the local authorities and the teacher unions sink their differences over curriculum control in the tri-partite Schools Council.
>
> Thus it was that the patrons and minders of the early innovators, or at least of the more eminent members thereof, saw the need to secure a future for them. Wheels turned and deals were struck. One of them led to the setting up of the Centre for Applied Research in Education (CARE) at the University of East Anglia, which (and this was thought to be a blessing at the time) had no school of education. This kind of package deal (tenured university posts for four people who didn't have two PhDs to rub together) implanted in higher education the 'seeds of its reconstruction' – in my view, the totally unintended but most significant and lasting impact of the curriculum development movement.
>
> (MacDonald 1991: 5–6)

CARE, then, provided a think-tank for curriculum development and school innovation and evaluation projects. The work was powered by the political settlements of the day and by the support of substantial elements in the liberal establishment, as well as the broader labour movement and other movements committed to social justice. At this time, then, educational researchers at CARE could act as public intellectuals since, in a sense, they were working with the grain of support from these social movements. It is always difficult to stand at one historical moment and recreate a sense of the past, but MacDonald has captured the heady sense of momentum in the early days of CARE:

> The curriculum development projects of the 1960s (by the end of the decade some two hundred national initiatives had been funded) led, in the 1970s, to a re-staffing of a still expanding system (the school leaving age was raised to 16 in 1972) on a new basis – the experience of change ... They poured into the departments of education in the universities and the polytechnics, the local authority advisory services, even the national inspectorate and senior school positions, bringing to

their new responsibilities a hands-on knowledge of the practice of schooling that would breathe new life into those atrophied institutions by challenging their traditions and offering them a new role. The beach-heads of an unfamiliar academic territory were rapidly established in higher education, increasingly under the title of 'curriculum studies'. The theoretical tradition of education based on derivative disciplines began to give way to the new theorists of educational practice whose theory was based on the close observation of new curricula in action, grounded theory of school life whose conceptual catholicity and seemingly casual disregard for the carefully constructed authority of the social sciences had to meet and survive accusations of amateurism and naive ignorance. But survive and flourish they did, not least because, supported by their colleagues in the local authority advisory services, they exerted an increasingly decisive role in the reshaping of in-service education for teachers, taking that opportunity to draw their students into the process of field-based enquiry into school problems and practices. That opportunity was extended as more and more colleges of initial training were incorporated into the institutions of higher education.

(MacDonald 1991: 6)

In such a climate as this the power of ideas is considerable. These initiatives represent a sense of 'a world under construction'. The public sector of schooling was being reconstructed and educational research provided important insights into this process. When public services are being reconceptualized and reconstructed in helpful and broadly supportive ways by sympathetic politicians, the educational researcher as public intellectual emerges from the shadows.

But this social democratic moment was about to be extinguished. In their powerful book, *Goodbye Great Britain*, Kathleen Burke and Alec Cairncross (1992) give an insider's view of the financial and economic events of 1976. Broadly speaking, the International Monetary Fund pronounced an end to the social projects of postwar Britain. But this was again part of a broader world movement that saw Western economies in the wake of the oil crisis of 1973 begin to struggle with new realities as the long postwar boom came to an end.

As we have seen, movements for social justice had developed sectors of support within the British establishment, but such a programme was never likely to win the hearts and minds of the rich and powerful, of those representing industrial and multinational interests. The advocates of the 'free market' emerged from the spawning think-tanks of the 1970s to define a programme that revised the projects of postwar Britain. The role of the public intellectual shifted towards these groups and, in doing so, left centres like CARE detached from the axes of power and policy. This crisis of positionality was to grow as the New Right programme gathered momentum and new adherents. CARE continued to function and to undertake major projects, but what was progressively lost was the link to an overarching social project which expressed the humanistic vision of the founding members. More and more research projects were generated in response to 'offers to tender', rather than conceived of for their public and moral purposes. New projects on police training, new technology and nurse training were undertaken. The rationales for such project work were forced to become more and more pragmatic and thereby less and less infused with broader visions of social justice.

The period of the 1980s and early 1990s has been described in various ways within CARE. One member argued that the project was 'to follow the fireball of New Right policies wherever they go . . . documenting and analysing the effects'. Another senior member at CARE noted with more humility that the Centre was going through a period of 'hibernation' but would, in due course, emerge from its burrow into the light of day.

In fact, in the 1980s, as has been noted, major proposals in the field of police training, in the health services, in the media, in libraries and in schools, were undertaken. The commitment to researching and evaluating the public services continued. As one member said, 'I've not given up on modernism yet!' Indeed, when I joined CARE in 1994 on sabbatical, and subsequently on a permanent basis, I was struck by the continuing force of the value system with regard to social justice and social projects. It was as if a collective memory of a more decent and compassionate Britain, what one described as 'a Britain that cares', continued to inform the work. But if the collective memory continued to provide moral guidance, what was palpable was the absence of social movements or indeed social moments in which to locate this value position. A hibernating collective memory grafted to a pragmatic programme of research and evaluation in a hostile world might summarize CARE in the 1990s. Like Sartre throughout his life, CARE appeared to be waiting . . .

The dominant motif of CARE in the 1990s was a series of pragmatic projects, still committed to and concerned with a basic vernacular humanism. What was missing was the overarching social movement that had been provided through the postwar egalitarian project. At one level one might say, in postmodern fashion, that all that was lost was a myth, a rhetoric of progress, a linear and unifying progress narrative, a masculinist, middle-class, mid-life, meritocratic, mythological muddle passing itself off as a high moral purpose. But, as I hope I have shown, the egalitarian project moved beyond discourses to mobilize and motivate substantial and influential sections of British society. We should, therefore, beware of limiting our understanding to discourse analysis and deconstruction, for it would be to misread and misrepresent a major period of reconstruction and struggle in British public life. The collective memory of that struggle still provides 'resources for hope' as we face the need to build new programmes and projects for millennial Britain. Specifically in CARE, the collective memory of humanistic egalitarianism remains strong and will infuse the search to reconstitute projects of social justice, although at the time of going to press new challenges are emerging to the continued existence of this centre.

Relocating public education

So, to summarize the previous section, the 'we're all in it together' socialism of the postwar governments settled into a balanced, partially egalitarian project until the mid-1970s. This temporary political settlement (which covered both parties for a time) allowed educational researchers to conduct policy-linked public intellectual work. It was the collapse of the egalitarian project which severed the link between public intellectual work and an overarching project of social justice. Although the collapse has taken place over the last twenty years, I believe we are only now beginning to face the implications and undertaking the task of rebuilding alliances and perspectives.

The implications for what Thompson called the *égalité* of this collapse of a social movement have been painfully rendered in an article Thompson wrote while in a National Health Service (NHS) ward, recovering from the disease that was ultimately to kill him:

> What makes me feel old, also, is the realisation that what I had thought to be widely held principles are now little more than quaint survivals among the least flexible of my generation. We had supposed, quite fiercely, that one didn't try to bend the rules. If people wanted to pay for convenience or for extras – good spectacles or special dentures or nursing home deliveries or convalescent comfort – we could go along with that. But access to the essential resources of the service must be ruled by *égalité*. And we believed that professional people (those who were socialists) should be loyal to this most of all. For if they started buying private latchkeys, then the whole system would start to get fouled up with the double standards and hierarchies of class. Times and manners have changed. The generation which fought for the NHS, and which has now come to that stage of life where they need it most, must jostle with the assertive anti-moralistic young. Everyone is into latch-keys, technicians and skilled workers as well. If my wife and I and a few friends want to hold out for old 'principles' no one is going to stop us. But I have to recognise now that such a stiff-backed sense of

honour could cost even risk to one's life. And if we still choose to be like that, can one possibly make the same choice for another – a child or a grandchild? And by what right?

One is left with a 'principle' that the young can't even understand, which is ineffectual (unless self-damaging), and which is really a private notion of honour. Or a stuffy habit of the old. And I suddenly can see the survivors of that socialist age-cohort as historical relics, like the old Covenantor in *The Heart of Midlothian*. Those of us who stay loyal to the old imperatives and taboos – the oaths of *égalité* – are a goldmine for the oral historian, and Raphael Samuel will collect us as specimens in a nostalgic book.

(Thompson 1987: 21)

The ritual death of the *égalité* at the hands of the market poses the classic problem of positionality for the humanistic public intellectual.

The nature of the crisis of positionality that emerged with the triumph of free markets is well illustrated in the cartoon reproduced in Figure 10.1. It shows in graphic detail the problems for humanistic caring professionals of trying to stand in the same place. At the beginning, in the first frame, the health professional inhabits a humane micro-world dispensing health service to *all* according to need – a vision of workaday socialist practice. By the end, that work has been repositioned into dispensing something else altogether. So a nurse may be working on the same ward, in the same hospital, throughout the two decades of Tory reconstruction, but by the end the positional significance of that work has been transformed. One would tell similar stories of probation officers, social workers, comprehensive school teachers and, indeed, educational researchers.

But let me return to Lawrence Stenhouse and to CARE, because it is here that we can interrogate some of the problems of positionality. During the 1970s, besides conducting a wide range of curriculum development and evaluation projects, CARE became a centre for defining educational research modalities in the public sphere. I have argued that egalitarian social movements offered aid and sustenance to educational research pursuing goals of social justice. But now the downside of this overarching social movement has to be confronted. For it is here we view the essential crisis of positionality – what might in another sense be called the *paradox of progressivism*.

Being interlinked and embedded in a wider political project for social justice, for an education of inclusion, a schooling that would seek to empower and enlighten all sections of society, produced its own blindnesses. For, as MacDonald (1991: 11) notes, 'We the innovators began under benign and supportive government and saw the problem largely as a technical one, under professional control.'

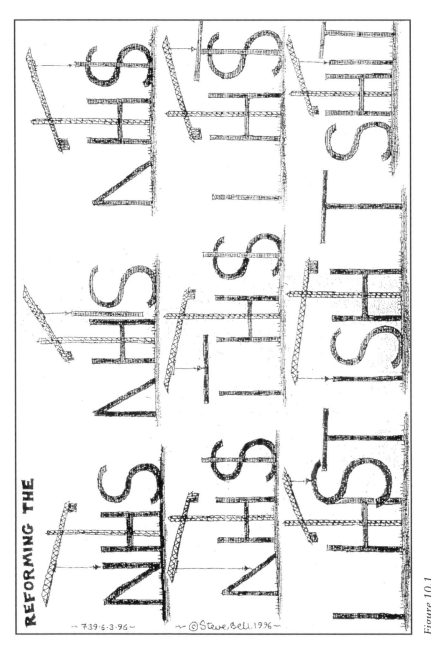

Figure 10.1
Source: Guardian, 6 March 1996: 16

The task for CARE, then, was to find intellectual answers to the problem of empowering education for all. This assumption of benign governance came from the salience of the egalitarian project in some establishment circles. CARE proceeded on a belief in good intentions, a secure sense of good faith and a belief in the moral high ground of work to educate all sections of society. This belief was to have profound consequences for it led into definitions of educational research that could be hijacked, perverted and repositioned for other social and political purposes. Because of the belief in governmental good intentions and in the ideological supremacy of egalitarianism, patterns of educational research remained depoliticized and detached from conceptualizations of power. Again, MacDonald has cogently reflected on the thirty-year moratorium which followed 1945:

> The development of a political consciousness in education was delayed by 30 years. The postwar expansion of schooling was powered by a political consensus around the notion of Keynesian social democracy (Marquand 1988). Throughout that period, it seemed that economic buoyancy would finance the agreed goals of full employment, adequate social services, and the co-existence of public and private enterprise. In 1970, expenditure on education exceeded expenditure on defence for the first, but last time. The writing was now on the wall (and the Schools Council under severe political attack as the warning signs were taken heed of) and recession looming. The consensus collapsed under Labour in the mid- to late-1970s in a massive failure of adaptation to the new economic realities. The truce was over, as was the indulgence. The politics of moderation were out, the politics of extremism in. The sense of a failing society (with schooling, of course, a favourite target) was pervasive, and of a failing socialism, conclusive. In an extraordinary ideological coup (not least of her own party), Thatcher seized the opportunity to introduce and implement a version of economic liberalism not seen since the nineteenth century – the undistorted market.
>
> (MacDonald 1991: 12)

This sense of good intentions led to a form of 'progressive overreach', whereby strong liberal and entrenched positions were overthrown in the search for more egalitarian, more inclusive modalities. In the progressive moment, confident of benign government, with an expansionist economy and social democratic movements seeking to counter the allure of communism, this *reaching for more* was profoundly understandable. Hence, 'applied research' was a central mantra of CARE in the early 1970s. Applied research sought to move beyond the liberal discourse of foundational theory in teacher education. In a paper on the future of CARE, Lawrence Stenhouse wrote:

> About fifteen years ago an attack was mounted on the intellectual standard of the teaching of education in universities and colleges. This

attack stressed the need to teach education through its *constituent disciplines*. Philosophy, psychology and sociology won a central place. History and comparative education were more peripheral. This attack carried the day and the majority of courses in education in both universities and colleges are now founded in the constituent disciplines.

The group working in CARE are united in a reaction against this, the predominant tradition at present. While not questioning the intellectual standard of the work being done in the constituent disciplines, we question its practical relevance. Holding that we understand too little of the educational process at policy, school and classroom levels, we are evolving methodologies for the study of the realities of educational systems. The emphasis is not unique to CARE, but I would claim that the CARE group is the most advanced unit of its kind in this country and that it has now developed a tradition which is characteristic.

(CARE 1974)

For the moment, I want to stay with Lawrence Stenhouse's diagnosis before returning to applied research as the solution. I have been spending a good deal of time thinking about the role of educational theory in schools of education. The focus on disciplined educational theory arose from the location of many schools of education within the university milieu (see Clifford and Guthrie 1988: 3–4, quoted in Chapter 2).

It was to solve some of these problems that Lawrence Stenhouse developed a notion of applied research. But I think the reaction to disciplinary theory went too far and, as we shall see, although no one could have foreseen this, the timing was bad. The issue was not to dismantle theory altogether, but to replace foundational theory with a more engaged theory/practice equation.

Applied research aimed to evacuate foundational theory to immerse itself in the realities of classroom life. In the process, however, the capacity of foundational and disciplinary theory to address broad questions about the historical, sociological and philosophical definition of schooling was potentially lost. Under benign governance, believing in good intentions – classrooms, compassionate and would-be democratic micro-worlds – these were the places to be and in which to conduct and generate applied research. What was lost in a welter of good intentions was the public intellectual handle on questions of the social position of schooling, the ideological content, the grammar, the social epistemology, the social and political place and purpose of schooling. Applied research in classrooms is fine when classrooms are progressing, becoming more inclusive, more democratic places. But when the tide turned, applied research suffered from extreme *discourse deficit*. The focus on application in classrooms left educational research a victim of those who could redefine applications and classrooms. Applied research was left with too few levers to look at the overarching questions once explored, albeit patchily, in foundational theory.

Moreover, the applied research movement, by aiding in the dissolution and deconstruction of foundational theory, helped soften up the context for a wholly different ideological coup of the sort referred to by MacDonald. By focusing back to practice, especially to classroom practices, the doors were open to a new, more utilitarian doctrine of teacher education and educational research. Teaching and schooling now could be presented as practical matters beyond broad intellectual contestation. And if teaching is a practical matter, then changing schooling is a matter of technical fine tuning and education research is only there to service the technical adjustments that will deliver effective schools.

The paradox of progressivism in the era of 1970s CARE is that by helping dismantle the liberal settlement of foundational and disciplinary theory to move towards a more engaged and practical applied research mode, a wholly different ideological coup was facilitated. By 1980, the forces that had long contested empowering education for all were in control, and their desire to extinguish educational theory which engaged questions of the nature and purposes of schooling was evident. For them, all arguments for applied and practical research aided in obscuring the larger question of social purpose and social allocation. Progressive arguments were hijacked, inverted and used for a wholly indifferent social project with diametrically opposed purposes.

Now in case this sounds too glib, which it does, and too critical of applied research, I should note that it is symptomatic of the broad-based paradox of progressivism in this period, of a crisis of positionality, not of one's own making and which could not have been fully foreseen. Certainly, I do not want to risk self-abuse, but I should note that much of my own work on school knowledge falls fairly and squarely into the positional trap I have defined, as do most other progressive modalities and practices conceived of in the thirty years since 1945. To say this is to confirm the extent of the task of reconceptualization and repositioning that stands before us. But there is a final paradox – while flawed and ultimately enmeshed in the positional trap defined earlier, the work of groups like CARE still provide the kind of collective memory and sets of working definitions and practices that will be invaluable in rebuilding new projects which aim at social justice and social enlightenment. As always, in social change we have to pick ourselves up and begin again, this time a little wiser, less believing in governmental and global good intentions, and more cognizant of the need for 'theories of evil' as we pursue our purposes.

So far, you may have discovered some modernist longing in this talk – so there is a whiff of the modernist dinosaur – but there is also a sense of the dangerous delusions of modernism which lead into so many positional

traps. Those dangerous delusions were sponsored in a period of expansionist economic reconstruction where more socially inclusive policies were
temporarily promised.

In this period, notions of the public sphere and of intellectual work, and
specifically education research which applied itself to improving public life,
were readily accessible. But in the last twenty years, there has been a profound struggle for public life and for the intellectual work associated with its
improvement. Lest we accept that it is a problem of shortage of money, it is
worth pointing out that the opposite is happening to the police, the army
and to expenditure on military weapons and private developments, like private shopping malls and private housing. Here there is a huge growth in
expenditure and in expanding developments. Overall, then, we are obviously not short of money. What is happening is that we are choosing con-
sistently the private over the public at nearly all levels, and this is playing
through into an attack on the 'median level'. Alan Wolfe (1996) argues that
the median levels of professional life are a confusing nuisance between the
direct relationship of the state and its subjects, and industry and its cus-
tomers. In the median level critique, social criticism, theory building and
arguments against inequality still reside.

The attempt, therefore, at the global level is to weaken this level and move
the centre of action for knowledge construction to other levels. Michael
Gibbons *et al.* (1994) have written about the distinction between Mode 1
and Mode 2 knowledge. Mode 1 knowledge is essentially disciplinary knowledge, normally developed in the traditional universities. Mode 2 knowledge
is applied knowledge, increasingly developed in the research and development sectors of the private industrial base, together with the think-tanks
associated with this sector of the economy. While Mode 1 knowledge
is under sustained attack, Mode 2 knowledge is being sponsored. This is
merely a version of the changing priority from the public to private that I
mentioned earlier.

One way to sidestep the whole question is to embrace the definition of
intellectuals provided in the *Dictionary of Scientific Quotations*. Tadeusz
Kotarbinski (1997: 2) is credited with the quotation, 'An intellectual is a
parasite that exudes culture.'

So if the public aspect of the public intellectual seems increasingly perilous
under postmodernity, let us examine the place of intellectuals more generally. In Britain this place has, of course, always been contested, whether
within modernity or after modernity.

Noel Annan (1995), though, considers that postwar academics enjoyed a
golden age of influence – he judges the period up until 1975 was the 'Age of
the Don'. Certainly, as we have seen in the case of CARE, there was for a
period a fruitful exchange between parts of the political establishment and
educational researchers – public policy and public intellectual work were

briefly linked. The link itself, of course, begs the question, for when the establishment changes tide, as happened in the 1970s, the role of public intellectual becomes instantly questionable in terms of the humanistic values expressed by those such as Stenhouse. Halsey has ruminated also on this matter in his book about the academy. He judges that British academics fall into two groups. The largest is a group who see themselves as increasingly specialist professions with a primarily conservative emphasis.

> First this somewhat heterogeneous collection of increasingly specialist professions is in a cultural sense conservative. This conservatism reflects in part the distinctive character of secure attachment to the State and the social order which has earned the description of the British 'key' profession as pragmatic and useful – a ready servant of government administration and industrial need.
>
> No one wishes to be labelled an intellectual, and worse, the intelligentsia is a dated, obscure class of foreign dissidents. Anti-intellectualism in this sense has been a feature of British culture at least since the reform and revival of the universities by the Victorians. The structure of British society has offered continually renewed support for these sentiments. There are professional rewards for specialists both within the academy and outside in the House of Lords, the boardrooms of industrial companies, the mass media, the governing bodies of quan-gos, and even the political parties. There have been, in short, powerfully integrating forces working to make scientists and scholars 'at home' in their society.
>
> (Halsey 1992: 247–8)

Halsey notes that what he calls the high professors, 'the leading one tenth of academic staff' (1992: 252), are disproportionately the highest qualified in terms of first class degrees and disproportionately more productive. They are also disproportionately linked to the establishment – a fifth of all high professors are privately schooled as opposed to 15 per cent of the general population. Halsey wrote:

> Oxford and Cambridge, with their close ties both in recruitment from the well-to-do and as suppliers to the elevated metropolitan institutions of State and Industry, are also dominantly the nurseries of both the intellectuals and the powers. Such a pattern of connection has undoubt-edly given Britain an integrated establishment of political, economic, and cultural management.
>
> (1992: 252)

Moreover, he notes that the high professors are to the right of their colleagues, 'both in their subjective place on the political spectrum and their voting record' (1992: 256).

However, Halsey also notes that, as always in British life, there exists across the academies what Orwell called 'the awkward squad' – a group that refuse hegemony for one reason or another, ranging from leftist commitment through to personal refusal.

Of course, it would be wrong to equate intellectuals with academics. But, since the word 'intellectual' first emerged in Russia to characterize the nihilistic university students, more and more intellectual life has been colonized by the massive expansion of universities. Edward Shils (1972: 3) describes intellectuals as 'persons with an unusual sensitivity to the sacred, an uncommon reflectiveness about the nature of their universe and the rules which govern their society'.

In the past, they have found patrons as disparate as royalty, the aristocracy, the church, the army, newspapers, the media, welfare and begging. But as Halsey (1992: 252) notes, nowadays we are forced to the conclusion that 'institutions of higher education are their major institutional location'.

Raymond Williams spent much of his life railing against the conservative bias of the academy, which he judged to be a central explanation of what he called 'English backwardness'. He makes the point that 'those who could be called intellectuals in other countries are in Britain mostly brought up in a system of private education designed for a class which includes the leading politicians, civil servants, company directors and lawyers' (Williams 1983).

Williams's diagnosis of late-1980s Britain is a depressing one:

At every level, including our own, this is a seriously undereducated society. The problems it faces are intractable with the kind of information and argument now publicly available. There is no obvious way of measuring this most serious of deficits. Some indications occur in the condition of our newspapers after a hundred years of general literacy, and in the character of parliamentary and electoral debates. The way is open for weak minds to renounce, in some despair, the whole project of public education.

(Williams 1989: 21)

Following Williams, let me then revisit the question of educational research, the public intellectual and, indeed, the issues of public education. For we face a contradiction. Halsey and Williams find an English intelligentsia which is either complicit with power or marginalized, but Annan (1995) reminds us that up until 1975 there was, in some sense, a golden age of influence. As we have seen, in the earlier examination of CARE this confluence was often on the side not of power but of social justice.

Clearly, the 'we're all in it together' socialism of the postwar governments settled into a balanced egalitarian project until the mid-1970s. This temporary political settlement (which covered both parties for a time) allowed educational researchers to conduct policy-linked public intellectual work. It was the collapse of the egalitarian project which served the link between public intellectual work and an overarching project of social justice.

In some ways, the changes to a market-based system challenge the very assumptions of postwar public life as, of course, they were intended to do. Public services wither, the public sector contracts and, in a broader sense, public life is diminished. This attack on things 'public' transforms the prospects for public life and public action. The attack on public space is intimately linked with the prospects of public intellectual engagement. Geoff Mulgan and Ken Worpole have spent a good deal of time surveying these changes and conclude:

> A profound change has overcome our public spaces. Only half the population now dares to go out after dark, fewer than a third of children are allowed to walk to school, and public fear of strangers regularly erupts after such public murders as Jamie Bulger and Rachel Nickell. Clearly this is not a nation at ease with itself.
>
> But while the parks, railway stations and many sidestreets are full of boarded up stalls, toilets and kiosks, billions of pounds have been pumped into glossy shopping centres such as Newcastle's Metro Centre and Sheffield's Meadowhall. Their virtue is that they offer security through control: no eating allowed except in designated spaces, no litter permitted, there is no weather, no running about and no dogs.
>
> (Mulgan and Worpole 1994: 24)

They might have added, as a US legal case confirmed, that since shopping malls are private space, no public political activities can be undertaken within them – hence a woman organizing a petition for a local community project was judged to be acting illegally. One begins to wonder what would be the status of an intellectual-cum-political conversation in a shopping mall – would this also be illegal? In the event, the owners have normally precluded such prospects – the muzak normally drives out the prospect of such talk, let alone thought. Suzanne Moore summarizes the effect of the changing public/private balance on a political and moral thought:

> The valorisation of private property that took place in the eighties produced an almost tangible disdain for anything that was not privately owned. As a psychic state, this was tolerable, but when people saw it enacted in their cities, schools and hospitals, the decay of public space, bad enough in itself, became symbolic of something even more rotten at the heart of the government. To talk of civic society, never mind civic duty, is difficult among broken-down playgrounds littered with old condoms and screwed-up tin foil, lifts that don't work, streets you wouldn't want your children to roam.
>
> (Moore 1994: 5)

In France, the dilemma can be more easily understood. In the Latin Quarter, intellectuals gathered in the postwar period around a cluster of bookshops, cafés and bars. Simone de Beauvoir, in her memoirs, captures this time when:

> Journalists, authors and would-be film-makers discussed, projected and decided with passion, as though their future depended upon them.
>
> But now the bookshops have been replaced with chic fashion stores. The cafés have likewise become chic, with industrialists and actors as the main clientele. Now the house prices are among the highest in Paris. The people who come here no longer belong to the academic world. They are people who earn a lot of money.
>
> (Quoted in Gauchet 1994: 20)

Marcel Gauchet, a philosopher and editor of the review *Le Debat*, says:

> The cafés are only the most visible aspect of this. The Sorbonne has completely changed and the students who go there are now entirely depoliticised: more than half the bookshops have shut, and the publishing houses are also leaving. For years this was the area that carried intellectual trends. Now, there might still be the odd author, the odd star, but there are no trends . . . The changes to the Latin Quarter reflect changes to the position of intellectuals in France and their obliteration from the political scene.
>
> (Gauchet 1994: 20)

Part of the problem of positionality and developing a strategy for renewal is how to reconnect with the project which began with the 'we're all in it together' spirit of the 1940s and continued in the egalitarian projects of the 1970s. Since 1979, this sense of collective social purpose has been under systematic attack.

In a crowded island, such a change in the ethos of the establishment has important implications for intellectuals located in the academy. For the quickest route to funds and fame has always been sucking up to the establishment, even becoming part of the educational establishment. Hedgers and trimmers always proliferate in such closely patrolled circumstances as exist in a small, crowded island. Since 1979 they have not just proliferated but have been honoured and promoted. As soon as the deeply flawed National Curriculum was pronounced, there were those who rushed forward with guides and how to implement this monument to iniquity. This form of collaboration has been richly rewarded.

But there was another feature of the crowded island which, I think, will return us inevitably to the compassionate 'there is such a thing as society' view, which underpins egalitarianism. It is, quite simply, very difficult to escape 'those dreadful people', as one Tory minister called the public who travel on British Rail. In *The Revolt of the Elites and the Betrayal of Democracy*, Lasch (1995) has shown how, in the USA, the elite – intellectuals included – have sought to escape all public commitments and public space. That option is not available on a crowded island – you can seek to demolish national rail services and national bus services, but the resulting traffic jams catch the rich as well as the poor. So in the end public transport will have to be reinvented and reinvigorated. It will prove to be the same with much of public life, which has been under assault for eighteen years. And with the revival of public life and public services, with the revival of that which is public, may come the revival of opportunities for would-be public intellectuals.

Reinventing public intellectual work as education

Broadly speaking, I have been dividing the experience of would-be public intellectuals into two forms. In the period of the 1960s and 1970s, those working for social justice undertook intellectual work against the background of a 'world under construction' – thought and action remained allied and the link to policy remained close enough for intellectuals to move beyond mere word games.

In the 1980s and early 1990s, those intellectuals working for social justice in education faced a 'world under deconstruction' – many of the most dearly held projects were dismantled or came under sustained attack. In this later period, detached from action and divorced from policy, the public intellectual was forced into an increasingly abstract position of arguing through words for policies and activities that were subject to discourses of disavowal, displacement and derision. This is a harsh terrain to occupy and yet there are many examples of people who continued to argue for social justice in race, gender and class terms.

I am reminded of a film I watched on the American Civil War. As the South was progressively defeated, less and less land was occupied – just a few towns and strips of land. In the end, the commentator said all that was left was a 'confederacy of the mind' – a collective memory of an aspiration.

In some ways, that has been the fate of movements for social justice and of associated intellectual work in the past two decades. But we should not underestimate the 'confederacy of the mind'. For one assertion I will make with great force is that the largest problem the attempted reconstruction of the past two decades has faced – the attempt to demolish the welfare state – is people's 'collective memory' of good public services, of commitments to provision for all, whether it be schools or hospitals. The vital task now is to reinvigorate, reenergize and reinvent new projects and programmes for social justice, for memories and predispositions in Britain remain remarkably resilient. We should now be looking to define a new role for the educational researcher in millennial Britain, and do so in ways informed by collective memories of social justice initiatives. This should, hopefully, presage a new investigation of the role of educational researcher as public intellectual, moving us into a new phase after the hopeful years of the 1960s and early 1970s and the reversal in the two decades that followed. Now we can hope again there are postmodern prospects to explore. I should note that I am not talking about re-establishing some old master narrative of social justice – more a set of voices and visions, a moving mosaic of intentions and plans.

Win Breines's distinction between prefigurative and strategic politics is relevant here. 'Prefigurative politics seeks to create and sustain within the lived practice of the movement relationships and political forms that "prefigure" and embody the desired society' (Breines 1980: 421). Work in NHS hospitals or in pioneering comprehensive schools might be such prefigurative sites. Here, involvement in policy and practice and the pursuit of ideals of social justice might all be pursued in tandem.

In the past twenty years, many of these prefigurative sites have been subject to severe disruption, if not dissolution. In these circumstances, prefigurative practice and policy are, to say the least, difficult. A kind of *piecemeal pragmatism* becomes the norm but without any energizing or inspiring overall visions. We are left working on bits of the mosaic but with no sense of what it might finally look like, or even if we will like the overall plan that emerges. Under *piecemeal pragmatism*, our public intellectual work often falls into the category of *micro-political contestation*, when we get involved in seeking to defend prefigurative practices or support those who are working to engender or maintain these practices and policies. Alternatives come when we involve ourselves in more traditional adversarial academic work by developing *critiques* of the rationales and routes of contemporary structures when driven by imperatives of the market.

This draws us back to Breines's second category of work – strategic politics. 'Strategic politics is concerned with building organisations in order to achieve power so that structural change in the political economic and social order might be achieved' (Breines 1980: 422). This work is now pressing, if new conceptions of service and education for social justice are to emerge, if new prefigurative activities and sites are to be created. For this to happen, our work must develop from past collective memory to defuse new visions and structures of education for achieving social justice. There are a number of places at which we might begin.

In terms of strategic politics, why might there be a chance of a new period for educational research? What are the grounds for hope? Well, just as I have argued that there was progressive overreach in the early 1970s, so I think there has been substantial *New Right overreach* in the past two decades.

Let me concentrate on three examples of overreach.

First, there has been the sustained attack on the professions and on public life generally. In some ways, in this period there has been a sustained attempt to alter the public/private balance in one society. The flux in the balance between public and private, between the state and civil society, makes it a particularly difficult time to arbitrate over the place of public intellectual work in educational research and elsewhere. In some ways, the changing balance echoes the American experience, famously summarized by Galbraith, as a move towards 'private wealth and public squalor'. Public life and institutions come under withering attack. The arguments of Wolfe (1996) carry considerable weight with me. Wolfe has argued that what we are seeing globally is an attack on what he calls the 'median level'. By 'median level', he means the public institutions: schools, universities, public broadcasting, libraries, hospitals and so on. In most countries, these institutions are coming under attack and this is evidenced by the fact that less and less is being spent on them.

John Gray has argued that a similar attack on median institutions (which Wolfe denotes) is at work in Britain:

> The Tory nationalisation of Britain's intermediary institutions – the universities, the NHS, even the prosecution service – has demolished the complex structure of checks and balances which we relied upon for protection against the abuse of power by the government of the day.
>
> (Gray 1995: 11)

Secondly, alongside the general attack on public life and specifically on the professions, there has been an erosion of local and community life. Powerful groups have disinvested in local communities and the effects on social fabric and life are clearly visible.

Thirdly, in the newspapers, television and more generally, the quality of public knowledge has been in substantial decline over the past two decades. As in the USA, *par excellence*, there has been a process of 'dumbing down' at work.

In each of these cases, however, there is evidence of *New Right overreach*. Let us take them in order, for they represent some of our opportunities to rejuvenate our public intellectual work. First, the attack on the professionals, specifically the attack on the teaching profession. In terms of strategic politics, the alliance between teachers and externally located researchers is potentially very powerful. This is because the teacher unions, certainly their leaders, now realize that the attack on educational research and theory is an attack on teachers' professionalism. Professional groups traditionally trade on their underpinning theoretical bodies of knowledge. Without these, they become technicians devoid of professional claims.

Research and theory and teacher unions, pursuing profession and status, desperately need each other.

This provides an important coalition for reworking the relationship and indeed the substance of theory and practice. This time we must avoid the estrangements of foundational theory and develop engaged practice-informing research and theory – especially new theories of educational inclusion. Above all, we must see that only when practice and new forms of theory come together can educational research hope to have any hold on defining educational visions and on planning new educational structures. We must grasp the central historical point that theory and practice are not inevitably or intrinsically divorced: it is structures and institutionalized missions that have created the divorce. But new structures and institutionalized practices could consummate a new marriage.

So we have to return to the point of rupture in the 1970s, where increasingly divorced educational theory led to calls for applied research and a return to practice. This rupture was hijacked to develop a whole-sale evacuation of theory and a return to classrooms and practice. From now on, the design of education was moved away from the intellectuals, the educationists, and firmly placed in the hands of politicians. Only new alliances between theory and practice can remake the possibility for educational research to contribute to new visions and new structures of education.

This could, then, be a beginning response to *New Right overreach* on the professions. What of the vacuum left in community life and public knowledge? Here there is the opportunity to define new strategies for curriculum and learning. If the National Curriculum concentrates on a uniform, unifying code divorced from local communities, the opportunity is open to develop new links between education and community building. What would a curriculum for community building look like, as opposed to one looking back to a mythical golden age of nationhood? The appeal of such a vision of education would, I think, be substantial and would highlight many of the iniquitous structures currently in place.

Likewise, at the level of public knowledge – the deterioration in public information offers new opportunities for educational research and activity – we are looking at the full implications of developing a learning society and improving public education both inside and, at least as crucially, outside the school. Here, we should be researching and defining new patterns – for public education in a learning society. Curriculum should focus on the pupil as researcher and not only as the passive recipient of other people's knowledge.

At this stage of a new government, new visions and voices in educational research are needed which harness some of the forces which were active at the time of the election. Without new visions we are stuck with the *piecemeal pragmatism* that has affected our work for two decades. We have to find new strategic politics and a way to create new prefigurative sites.

Moreover, as the new government increases its call for a more professional teaching force, the alliance between research and theoretical knowledge and teaching will once again be forced on to the agenda. This time, we have to be ready with a range of new collaborative perspectives and activities. These new perspectives need to stress educational research which acts as a kind of *moral witness* to the initiatives that are undertaken. Hopefully, we can once again join in a world under construction, and this time our intellectual inauguration needs to envision a *new moral order* for schooling.

With this new moral order, let me return you to Lawrence Stenhouse's last lecture. Here, he asked the question whether learning and critical literacy should be confined to an elite:

> Our system [he said] is notable for being in the power of those who do not commit their own children to it and it is accordingly vulnerable. The powerful still do not favour the cultivation among the lower orders of the scepticism and critical intelligence that is valued among their betters. It is for that reason that they point backwards to basics in the face of the potential of the exciting curricula in literacy and numeracy and knowledge to be found in the recent curriculum movement, in the leading state schools and in the more enlightened private schools.
>
> At stake is more than 100 years of adventure beyond the mere basics, a span in which schools have – fitfully no doubt – tried to make people independent thinkers capable of participation in the democratic process and of deciding what the future of their society shall be like. Perhaps a faith in expansion and progress underlay that provision for the citizen. We must now find ways of ensuring that a defensive, and more apprehensive, establishment in the context of a contracting economy does not make a critical education an education reserved for privilege.
>
> (Quoted in Simon 1990: 19–20)

In ending with Lawrence Stenhouse's quote, we see how our collective memory of a humane society continues to infuse our search for a new moral order for schooling and education.

eleven

Educational change and the crisis of professionalism (with Andy Hargreaves)

In his new book on the changing structure of television, the French sociologist Pierre Bourdieu (1998) explores the vast forces of the 'market' in restructuring the content and delivery of television programmes. Television, he shows, is being 'dumbed down'; its content is being restructured, its social and educational mission degraded. Occupying a position of some ambivalence in relation to this restructuring project are the professionals – the journalists, interviewers and programme makers. These 'peer groups', as Bourdieu terms them, have the capacity either to blindly administer market commands or, alternatively, to respond in a more micro-political peer group manner. By its very nature, the latter pattern is semi-autonomous.

Professional groups through their practices cannot be completely integrated. This perhaps explains the absence of support, notably financial, for professional groups initiated by the agencies of global corporations over the past decade. Professional peer groups still retain considerable power to 'interfere' in the relationship between corporate businesses and consumers, and the state and its citizens.

Looking at education, we can investigate the power to restructure teaching practices and peer group professional activities at a number of levels. First, there is the traditional route of the 'status and resources game' played out in the universities and colleges which define education as a field. This is what we might call the academicization project. Secondly, there is activity at the level of teaching. Here, there is the traditional route of the professionalization project: the pursuit of status and resources for an occupational group. Professionalization has to be set against professionalism, which is the other side of the coin – teachers' definition of their peer group practices, their best ways of pursuing the art and the craft of teaching. Sometimes, professionalization and professionalism are in harmony, sometimes not. At times like this, when global forces are pursuing stratification projects, harmony between the two is unlikely. But, like Bourdieu's peer group, teachers' professionalism can stand against restructuring forces if those forces run counter to their own professional and moral purposes. This can be achieved by working for and defining a new moral professionalism.

For that reason, I want to focus in this chapter on the possibilities that exist in the contemporary situation for developing and defending a new moral professionalism – what I call a principled professionalism.

Let me continue, then, by extending our analyses of two distinctions: the distinction between professionalization and professionalism, and the distinction between professional standardization and professional standards.

Beginning with the distinction between professionalization and professionalism or professionality, I see the project of professionalization as concerned with promoting the material and ideal interests of an occupational group – in this case, teachers. Alongside this, professionalism is more concerned with the intricate definition and character of occupational action – in this case, the practice and profession of teaching. At the moment, we see considerable antipathy to teacher professionalization. This opposition comes from cost-cutting central government; from well-entrenched education bureaucracies; and perhaps, most potently of all, from a range of business and corporate interests. Some of the reasons for the opposition to teacher professionalization are undoubtedly ideological, but behind this ideological antipathy are a range of financial changes which sponsor the notion of retrenchment and cutback. Now, as a number of commentators have pointed out, the relationship between ideology and financial manipulation is a historically intimate one. But, in this case, it is possible to distinguish between real financial constraints and their linkage to ideological opposition to professionalization as a social and political project.

In the opposition to professionalization, there is currently considerable activity, both administratively and politically, in the definition and application of professional standards of practice. While these initiatives and edicts are often aimed at curbing the professionalization project, they do nonetheless sponsor new opportunities for developing teacher professionalism.

Let me explain this double-sided face of educational change by looking at the distinction between standards and standardization. The contradiction at work in school changes at the moment is that standardization is dominant. Teacher professionalism is being driven by more and more government guidelines and central edicts, on issues ranging from assessment to accountability to curriculum definition. In the process, it would seem that teaching is being technicized but not professionalized. In fact, such standardization is unpicking existing patterns of professionalization and replacing them with notions of the teacher as the technical deliverer of guidelines and schemes devised elsewhere.

At the same time, there is a desire to promote and improve professional standards. Since a major plank of governmental and business rhetoric about education is that schooling will improve, a focus on professional standards becomes a logical extension of this project. So there can be simultaneously opposition to professionalization and sponsorship of new patterns of professionalism. In a sense, this dichotomy is the one between control and delivery. The new accommodation being pushed for by central governments and corporate interests is that the objectives and patterns of control are defined, but the management and delivery, and indeed the professional standards, are left to regulation by the occupational group.

What these two different spectra point to – professionalization alongside professionalism, and standardization alongside standards – is that the current condition of teachers' professional lives is paradoxical. There is both a desire for standardization of teaching and antipathy to the professionalization project, but this stands in harmony with a desire for greater professional standards and professionalism. Our task, it seems to me, is to build on the new spaces and possibilities offered by the second set of desires: the wish for higher standards and greater professionalism. Just at the commonsensical level, it is possible to argue against the material aggrandizement of professional groups, and this can be done both ideologically and financially, and, indeed, is being done at the moment. But, at the same level, it is enormously hard for groups in government bureaucracy or corporations to argue against professional standards and greater professionalism. Hence, our leverage in promoting new professionalism is potentially substantial.

Writing recently about primary school teachers, Troman (1996) differentiated between two kinds of professional groups of teachers. The first of these he calls the old professionals, who believed in teachers' collective control of their work and in resisting hierarchical control, whether in the school by principals or outside by administrators, bureaucrats and politicians. Against this group, he sets the new professionals who accept the new political dispensation and hierarchies, new governmental guidelines and new national objectives and curriculum, but who, nonetheless, in defining their professional practices, do so in a semi-autonomous and often progressive way. (In some ways, I am reminded of the British distinction between Old Labour and Tony Blair's New Labour – the latter clearly accepts new global hierarchies and patterns of control, but aims to define autonomous spaces in the 'New World Order'.)

My own sense is that if the attack on old professionals can be seen as deprofessionalization, the definitions of the new professionals can be seen as shifting the ground to defining new professionalisms (possibly setting the ground, therefore, for a new reprofessionalization project). At the moment, however, both the old and the new professionals must attempt to reappropriate professionalization projects at the level of professional practices. The ground for hopeful action is in defining new professional practices.

In this chapter, I discuss three ages and stages of professionalism: classical, practical and principled. This has some parallels with Hargreaves's (2000) 'Four ages of professionalism and professional learning'. Traditionally, academicization projects, professionalization projects and associated professionalisms have been linked, in what Andy Hargreaves and I have previously called 'classical professionalism' (Hargreaves and Goodson 1996: 4–9): 'This academic quest to develop and clarify a knowledge base for teaching tries to build an edifice of teacher professionalism and professionalisation on a foundation of *scientific certainty*' (1996: 6), by categorizing and codifying the practical knowledge of teachers in technical, scientific or theoretical terms.

In classical professionalism, then, the pursuit of status and resources open up an inevitable rift between educational study and research and practice. This is the price of pursuing professionalization through academicization.

In the period of recent free market dominance, marketization has tended to replace academic mystification as the route to professionalization. Here the professional is the trained expert who will deliver, with technical and scientific facility, the guidelines and reforms as defined by policy makers, administrators and politicians. The free market professional gives up some powers of definition and autonomy, but is handsomely rewarded in the new financial arrangement required of the market, which provides for incentives and discretionary payments for those defined as leaders, managers and, in England, so-called 'super-teachers'.

As I argued in the previous section, the terrain over which the new struggles are being waged is moving from the higher levels of the academic marketplace and the free marketplace to the long-contested area of professional practices. A number of phases can be seen emerging in the new struggles over professional practices.

An interim phase is likely to be an attempt to define practical professionals. This phase can be discerned in a range of countries at the moment, and it is one with a number of hopeful characteristics but, as we shall see, with a substantial downside. Practical professionalism tries to accord dignity and status to the practical knowledge and judgement that people have of their own work. This approach is 'designed to capture the idea of experience in a way that allows us to talk about teachers as knowledgeable and knowing persons' (Connelly and Clandinin 1988: 25). The reliance on experience that was once seen as a failing of teachers is regarded here as central to their expertise and, in its own way, as a source of valid theory, rather than theory's opposite or enemy. The routine and situated knowledge that teachers have of curriculum materials and development, subject matter, teaching strategies, the classroom milieu, parents and so forth – these are the sorts of phenomena that make up the substance of teachers' personal practical knowledge or craft knowledge (Brown and McIntyre 1993). Such knowledge can also be captured and communicated in particular forms, especially through images, metaphors, narratives and stories which teachers routinely use to represent their work to themselves and others.

One very helpful addition to the discourse of practical professionalism is the notion of reflective practice. The concept of the 'reflective practitioner' was pioneered and developed by the late Donald Schön (1983) as a way of describing and developing skilled and thoughtful judgement in professions like teaching. Reflection here means thinking which is not just ivory-towered contemplation, but is linked directly to practice (Grimmett and Erickson 1988; Grimmett and Mackinnon 1988). The heart of professionalism in this perspective is the capacity to exercise discretionary judgement in situations of unavoidable uncertainty (Schön 1983).

Schön's work provides a useful basis for future work on moral professional practices. Teacher educators have not been slow to pick up the implications of his work. They have shown how all teaching embodies reflection or thoughtful judgement within the actual practice of teaching itself (Pollard and Tann 1987). They have tried to investigate how teachers might best represent and explain their practice reflectively to one another, especially between more and less experienced peers. Some have moved beyond the more technical aspects of reflection regarding the details of classroom judgement – beyond *reflection-in-action* and *reflection-on-action*, that is – to argue for more critical *reflection about action*, and about the social conditions and consequences of one's actions as a teacher (e.g. Carr and Kemmis 1983; Elliot 1991; Fullan and Hargreaves 1991: 67–9; Liston and Zeichner 1991). Clearly, there are many purposes and ways of reflecting, not just one (Louden 1991). But what matters throughout this literature are the emphases that all teachers reflect in some way: that they can articulate and share their reflections more explicitly; that reflection is at the heart of what it means to be professional; and that teacher education, supervision and development should be constructed in ways that make such explicit reflection more feasible and more thorough.

At its best, the discourse of practical and reflective professionalism superbly deconstructs the intellectual pretensions of university-based, scientific knowledge as a basis for teacher professionalization. At its most critical, it also connects the practical reflection of teachers to broader social agendas of equity and emancipation, making practical reflection social and critical, as well as personal and local. But when it assumes extremely personalized and romantic forms, the discourse of practical professionalism is open to a damaging dual criticism.

The first critique is obvious and commonsensical, for not all teachers' practical knowledge is educational, beneficial or socially worthwhile. For instance, some teachers' practical knowledge 'tells' them that mixed ability teaching is not workable or appropriate (Hargreaves 1996); that children cannot be trusted to evaluate their own work; or that sciences are more suitable for boys than girls. If teacher professionalism is to be understood as exercising reflective judgement, and developing and drawing on a wide repertoire of knowledge and skills to meet goals of excellence and equity within relationships of caring, then whether practical knowledge can provide a proper foundation for it depends on what that knowledge is, in what kinds of contexts it has been acquired, the purposes to which it is put, and the extent to which teachers review, renew and reflect on it.

A second line of criticism is that over-zealous promotion of teachers' everyday, practical craft knowledge (albeit for the best-intended reasons) may actually redirect their work away from broader moral and social projects and commitments. In this sort of scenario, right-of-centre governments can restructure teachers' work and teacher education in ways that narrow such work to pedagogical skills and technical competencies, remove from teachers any moral responsibility or professional judgement concerning curricular matters, and cut teachers off from university knowledge with the access it can give to independent inquiry, intellectual critique and understanding of other teachers in other contexts. This can transform practical knowledge into parochial knowledge. Some of the more excessive swings towards school-based training and professional development schools threaten just this sort of transformation.

Furthermore, practical knowledge also limits the development of teachers' cognitive maps of power. Martin Lawn has written powerfully about how teachers' work in England and Wales has been restructured along just these lines:

> In the biographies of many teachers is an experience of, and exception of, curriculum responsibility not as part of a job description, a task, but as part of the moral craft of teaching, the real duty. The post-war tradition of gradual involvement in curriculum responsibility at primary and second level (in England and Wales) was the result of the wartime breakdown of education, the welfare aspects of schooling and the post-war reconstruction in which teachers played a pivotal, democratic role. The role of teaching expanded as the teachers expanded the role. In its ideological form within this period, professional autonomy was created as an idea. As the post-war consensus finally collapsed and corporatism was demolished by Thatcherism,

teaching was again to be reduced, shorn of its involvement in policy and managed more tightly. Teaching is to be reduced to 'skills', attending planning meetings, supervising others, preparing courses and reviewing the curriculum. It is to be 'managed' to be more 'effective'. In effect, the intention is to depoliticize teaching and to turn the teacher into an educational worker. Curriculum responsibility now means supervising competencies.

(Lawn 1990: 389)

Lawn's analysis points to the need for macro-level understanding of the implications of initiatives which, advertently or inadvertently, may redirect teacher professionalization into dark corners or cul-de-sacs. In many places, teacher professionalism is being redefined in terms of workplace competencies and standards of pedagogical practice, while teachers are having moral responsibility for curriculum goals and purposes taken away from them, financial resources are being withdrawn from them, and market ideologies of choice, competition and self-management are restructuring school systems and students' lives inequitably all around them.

The promise of practical professionalism, then, is that it can usefully invert and subvert the elitism and esotericism of university-based knowledge as a basis for teacher professionalization. Practical wisdom, developed in suitable contexts, for worthwhile purposes, in appropriately reflective ways, can and should form an important part of what it means to be professional as a teacher. But embraced exclusively and to excess, practical professionalism is easily hijacked in the service of dubious policy projects which restructure education inequitably, and narrow the teacher's task and the teacher's professionalism to delivering the goals of that restructured system technically, competently but unquestioningly. In this sense, we feel the rise of practical professionalism may threaten to move us into a period of *deprofessionalizing professionalism* where more narrow, technical definitions of professionalism, emptied of critical voice or moral purpose, seriously damage teachers' long-term aspirations for greater professional status and recognition.

To move beyond a deprofessionalizing practicalism, we need to investigate new attempts to unite professional practices with more practically sensitive theoretical studies and research modes. This would provide both new and up-to-date professional practices, backed up and informed by theory and research. What is required is a new professionalism and body of knowledge driven by a belief in social practice and moral purpose. Principled professionalism might cover the following issues listed below and would grow from the best insights of the old collective professionals and the new professionals. What teacher professionalism should also mean in a complex, postmodern age has been defined by Hargreaves and myself in our book, *Teachers' Professional Lives* (Goodson and Hargreaves 1996). We outlined seven components, which are set out below, of what we call post-modern professionalism, as exemplifying the principled professionalism I advocate in this chapter:

- first, and most importantly, opportunities and expectations with regard to engaging with the *moral and social purposes* and value of what teachers teach, along with major curriculum and assessment matters in which these purposes are embedded;
- increased opportunity and responsibility for exercising *discretionary judgement* concerning the issues of teaching, curriculum and care that affect one's students;
- commitment to working with colleagues in *collaborative cultures* of help and support as a way of using shared expertise to solve the ongoing problems of professional practice, rather than engaging in joint work as a motivational device to implement the external mandates of others;
- occupational *heteronomy* rather than self-protective *autonomy*, whereby teachers work authoritatively, yet openly and collaboratively with other partners in the wider community (especially parents and students themselves), who have a significant stake in students' learning;
- a commitment to active *care* and not just anodyne *service* for students. Professionalism must in this sense acknowledge and embrace the emotional as well as the cognitive dimensions of teaching, and also recognize the skills and dispositions that are essential to committed and effective caring;
- a self-directed search and struggle for *continuous learning* related to one's own expertise and standards of practice, rather than compliance with the enervating obligations of *endless change* demanded by others (often under the guise of continuous learning or improvement);
- the creation and recognition of high *task complexity*, with levels of status and reward appropriate to such complexity. (Goodson and Hargreaves 1996: 20–1)

In a new moral order of teaching, professionalization and professionalism will unite around moral definitions of teaching and schooling. Principled professionalism will develop from clearly agreed moral and ethical principles. This kind of professionalism will focus on the caring concerns which should lie at the heart of professionalism, rather than the contradictory and narrow concerns of professionalization. The latter have tended to focus on the material conditions and status concerns of teachers as a professional group. Principled professionalism will return to the initial concerns which underpin the profession of teaching. Teaching is, above all, a moral and ethical vocation, and a new professionalism needs to reinstate this as the guiding principle.

In other places, these debates have begun to surface with some force. Elizabeth Campbell has logically argued that in our lives:

> Teachers need to establish and enforce acceptable ethical standards in order to be self-regulating and accountable as professionals. Teachers also need ethical standards that can act as a guide and resource to help them cope with the ethical complexities and dilemmas inherent in the practice of teaching.
>
> (Campbell 2000: 218)

Campbell provides a valuable contextual background to this view and shows that it is a concern that has been voiced at other times in different socio-political circumstances. Campbell quotes the Minister of Education in Ontario, 1915:

> No profession can really exist without a code of ethics to guide the conduct of its members. Doctors, lawyers, and clergymen have their ethical codes, but teachers can scarcely be said to have such a code. Until they have developed a professional spirit which is characterized by loyalty to their recognized ethical standards, they cannot rank with the learned professions.
>
> (2000: 203)

Once the moral and ethical vocation of teaching is elevated to a priority, it becomes clear that importing business methods of research, accountability and performance pay are peculiarly ill-suited methods. Ethics and morality have never been major concerns in business procedures: here the legitimate concern is to make money. For this reason, above all, the rehabilitation of a new form of principled professionalism brings with it the associated need for more sensitive modes of research study and theory building. Following these routes, a new moral order of schooling might once again be pursued, and the professional personnel involved in its delivery might be accorded the respect and sensitivity that they and their pupils so urgently deserve.

References

Acker, S. (ed.) (1989) *Teachers, Gender and Careers*. London: Falmer Press.

Acker, S. (1994) *Gendered Experience*. Buckingham: Open University Press.

Acker, S. (1999) *The Realities of Teachers' Work*. London: Cassell.

Andrews, M. (1991) *Lifetimes of Commitment: Ageing, Politics, Psychology*. Cambridge: Cambridge University Press.

Annan, N. (1995) *Our Age: The Generation that Made Postwar Britain*. London: HarperCollins.

Armstrong, P. (1987) *Qualitative Strategies in Social and Educational Research: The Life History Method in Theory and Practice*, Newland Papers no. 14. Hull: School of Adult and Continuing Education, University of Hull.

Arnold, S. (2001) Savage angels, *Observer Review*, 4 February: 12.

Ball, S. and Goodson, I. (eds) (1985) *Teachers' Lives and Careers*. London: Falmer Press.

Becker, H. (1970) *Sociological Work: Method and Substance*. Chicago, IL: Aldine.

Becker, H. and Geer, B. (1971) Latent culture: a note on the theory of latent social roles, in B. Cosin *et al.* (eds) *School and Society: A Sociological Reader*. London: Routledge and Kegan Paul.

Ben-David, T. and Collins, R. (1966) Social factors in the origins of a new science: the case of psychology, *American Sociological Review*, 31(4): 451–65.

Berg, A. (1989) *Goldwyn. A Biography*. New York, NY: Knopf.

Bleasdale, A. and Self, D. (eds) (1985) *Boys from the Blackstuff*. Gloucester: Nelson Thornes.

Bly, R. (1991) *Iron John*. Shaftesbury: Element Books.

Bourdieu, P. (1998) *In Television and Journalism*. London: Pluto Press.

Breines, W. (1980) The New Left and Michele's 'Iron Law' social problems, *Community and Organisation*, 27(4): 419–29.

Bristow, J. (1991) Life stories. Carolyn Steedman's history writing, *New Formations*, 13: 113–30.

Brooks, R. (1992) 'And finally . . .' *News at Ten* goes tabloid, *The Observer*, 19 July: 69.

Brown, S. and McIntyre, D. (1993) *Making Sense of Teaching*. Buckingham: Open University Press.

Bucher, R. and Strauss, A. (1976) Professions in process, in M. Hammersley and P. Woods (eds) *The Process of Schooling: A Sociological Reader*. London: Routledge and Kegan Paul.

Bullough, R. (1989) *First Year Teacher: A Case Study*. New York, NY: Teachers College Press.

Bullough, R. (1998) Musings on life writing: biography and case study in teacher education, in C. Kridel (ed.) *Writing Educational Biography: Explorations in Qualitative Research*. New York, NY: Garland.

Bullough, R., Knowles, G. and Crow, N. (1991) *Emerging as a Teacher*. London: Routledge.

Burke, K. and Cairncross, A. (1992) *Goodbye Great Britain: The 1976 IMF Crisis*. New Haven, CT: Yale University Press.

Buruma, I. (1991) Signs of life, *The New York Review of Books*, 38(4): 3–4.

Butt, R., Raymond, D., McCue, G. and Yamagishi, L. (1992) Collaborative autobiography and the teacher's voice, in I. Goodson (ed.) *Studying Teachers' Lives*. London: Routledge.

Campbell, E. (2000) Professional ethics in teaching: towards the development of a code of practice, *Cambridge Journal of Education*, 30(2): 203–21.

CARE (Centre for Applied Research in Education) (1974) Unpublished paper on the future of the Centre for Applied Research in Education. CARE, University of East Anglia, 28 October.

Carr, W. and Kemmis, S. (1983) *Becoming Critical: Knowing Through Action Research*. London: Falmer Press.

Carter, K. (1993) The place of story in the study of teaching and teacher education, *Educational Researcher*, 22(1): 5–12.

Casey, K. (1988) Teacher as author: life history narratives of contemporary women teachers working for social change. Unpublished PhD dissertation, University of Wisconsin.

Casey, K. (1992) Why do progressive women activists leave teaching? Theory, methodology and politics in life-history research, in I. Goodson (ed.) *Studying Teachers' Lives*. London: Routledge.

Casey, K. and Apple, M. (1989) Gender and the conditions of teachers' work: the development of understanding in America, in S. Acker (ed.) *Teachers, Gender and Careers*. London: Falmer Press.

Chambers, C. (1991) Review of teachers as curriculum planners: narratives of experience, *Journal of Education Policy*, 6(3): 353–4.

Chomsky, N. (1995) A rebel with an endless cause, *Times Higher Education Supplement*, 23 June: 17.

Clandinin, D. and Connelly, F. (1998) Asking questions about telling stories, in C. Kridel (ed.) *Writing Educational Biography: Explorations in Qualitative Research*. New York, NY: Garland.

Clifford, G. and Guthrie, J. (1988) *Ed School: A Brief for Professional Education*. Chicago, IL: University of Chicago Press.

Cochran-Smith, M. and Fries, M. (2001) Sticks, stones and ideology: the discourse of reform in teacher education, *Educational Researcher*, 30(8): 3–15.

Cochran-Smith, M. and Lytle, S. (1999) The teacher research movement: a decade later, *Educational Researcher*, 28(7): 15–25.

Connelly, F. and Clandinin, D. (1988) *Teachers as Curriculum Planners: Narratives of Experience*. New York, NY: Teachers College Press.

Csikszentmihalyi, M. (1991) *Flow: The Psychology of Optimal Experience*. New York, NY: HarperCollins.

Dehli, K. (1994) Subject to the new global economy: power and positioning in Ontario labour market policy formation, in R. Priegert Coulter and I. Goodson (eds) *Rethinking Vocationalism: Whose Work/life Is It?*. Toronto: Our Schools/ Ourselves.

Denzin, N. (1989) *Interpretative Biography*, Qualitative Research Methods, Series 17. London: Sage Publications.

Denzin, N. (1992) Deconstructing the biographical method. Paper presented to the American Educational Research Association Annual Meeting, San Francisco, April.

Denzin, N. (1993) Review essay: on hearing the voices of educational research. Mimeo, University of Illinois at Urbana-Champaign, Illinois.

Denzin, N. and Lincoln, Y. (eds) (2000) *Handbook of Qualitative Research*, 2nd edn. Thousand Oaks, CA: Sage.

DES (Department of Education and Science) (1992) *Initial Teacher Training (Secondary Phase)*. Circular 9/92, para. 14. London: DES.

Dionne, E. (1992) The disillusion with politics could be dangerous, *Guardian Weekly*, 19 July: 18.

Dollard, J. (1949) *Criteria for the Life History*. Magnolia, MA: Peter Smith.

Eco, U. (1986) *Travels in Hyper Reality*. San Diego, CA: Harcourt Brace Jovanovich.

Elliot, J. (1991) *Action Research for Educational Change*. Buckingham: Open University Press.

Fine, M. (1994) Working the hyphens: reinventing self and others in qualitative research, in N. Denzin and Y. Lincoln (eds) *Handbook of Qualitative Research*. London: Sage Publications.

Fink, D. (2000) *Good Schools/Real Schools: Why School Reform Doesn't Work*. New York, NY: Teachers College Press.

Fullan, M. (1987) Implementing educational change: what we know. Paper prepared for the World Bank, Washington, DC.

Fullan, M. (1991) *Productive Educational Change*. London: Falmer Press.

Fullan, M. (1999) *Change Forces: The Sequel*. London: Falmer Press.

Fullan, M. (2000) The return of large-scale reform, *Journal of Educational Change*, 1(1): 5–28.

Fullan, M. and Hargreaves, A. (1991) *What's Worth Fighting For? Working Together for Your School*. Toronto: Ontario Public School Teachers' Federation.

Fullan, M. and Park, P. (1981) *Curriculum Implementation: A Resource Booklet*. Toronto: Ontario Ministry of Education.

Fullan, M. and Stiegelbauer, S. (1991) *The New Meaning of Educational Change*, 2nd edn. London: Cassell.

Gardner, H. (1993) *Creating Minds*. New York, NY: Basic Books.

Gauchet, M. (1994) Maman saps the soul of Sartre's city, *The Observer*, 18 September: 20.

Gibbons, M., Limoges, C., Nowotny, H., Schwartzman, S., Scott, P. and Trow, M. (1994) *The New Production of Knowledge*. London: Sage Publications.

Giddens, A. (1991) *Modernity and Self-Identity: Self and Society in the Late Modern Age*. Stanford, CA: Stanford University Press.

Giddy, D. (1807) *The Parliamentary Debates – Parochial Schools Bill*, 2nd reading, Vol. IX, 13 July. London: Hansard.

Giroux, H. (1991) *Border Crossings*. London: Routledge and Kegan Paul.

Goleman, D. (1995) *Emotional Intelligence*. New York, NY: Bantam Books.

Goodson, I. (1981) Life histories and the study of schooling, *Interchange*, 11(4): 62–76.

Goodson, I. (1991) Sponsoring the teacher's voice: teachers' lives and teacher development, *Cambridge Journal of Education*, 21(1): 35–45.

Goodson, I. (ed.) (1992) *Studying Teachers' Lives*. London: Routledge.

Goodson, I. (1993) Forms of knowledge and teacher education, in P. Gilroy and M. Smith (eds) *International Analyses of Teacher Education, JET Papers 1*, 19(465): 217–29.

Goodson, I. (1994a) Studying the teacher's life and work, *Teaching and Teacher Education*, 10(1): 29–37.

Goodson, I. (1994b) *Studying Curriculum: Cases and Methods*. Buckingham: Open University Press.

Goodson, I. (1995a) Education as a practical matter: some issues and concerns, *Cambridge Journal of Education*, 25(2): 137–48.

Goodson, I. (1995b) Teachers' life histories and studies of curriculum and schooling, in I. Goodson (ed.) *The Making of Curriculum: Collected Essays*, 2nd edn. London: Falmer Press.

Goodson, I. (1995c) *The Making of Curriculum: Collected Essays*, 2nd edn. London: Falmer Press.

Goodson, I. (1999) The educational researcher as a public intellectual, *British Educational Research Journal*, 25(3): 277–97.

Goodson, I. (2001) Social histories of educational change, *Journal of Educational Change*, 2(1): 45–63.

Goodson, I. and Ball, S. (1984) *Defining the Curriculum: Histories and Ethnographies*. London: Falmer Press.

Goodson, I. and Cole, A. (1993) Exploring the teacher's professional knowledge, in D. McLaughlin and B. Tierney (eds) *Naming Silenced Lives*. London: Routledge.

Goodson, I. and Fliesser, C. (1994) Exchanging gifts: collaborative research and theories of context, *Analytic Teaching*, 15(2): 41–6.

Goodson, I. and Foote, M. (2001) Testing times: a school case study, *Education Policy Analysis Archives*, 9(2), 15 January. (http://epaa.asu.edu/epaa/v9n2.html)

Goodson, I. and Hargreaves, A. (eds) (1996) *Teachers' Professional Lives*. London: Falmer Press.

Goodson, I. and Sikes, P. (2001) *Life History Research in Educational Settings: Learning from Lives*. Buckingham: Open University Press.

Goodson, I. and Walker, R. (1991) *Biography, Identity and Schooling: Episodes in Educational Research*. London: Falmer Press.

Gray, J. (1995) Bite of the New Right, *Guardian*, 23 October: 11.

Green, C. (2001) The railwayman's lament, *Guardian*, 14 April: 28.

Greene, M. (1991) Retrieving the language of compassion: the education professor in search of community, *Teachers College Record*, 92(4): 541–55.

Grimmett, P. and Erickson, G. (1988) *Reflection in Teacher Education*. New York, NY: Teachers College Press.

Grimmett, P. and Mackinnon, A. (1988) Craft knowledge and the education of teachers, *Review of Research in Education*, 18: 385–456.

Hall, G. and Hord, S. (1987) *Change in Schools; Facilitating the Process*. Albany, NY: State University of New York Press.

Halsey, A. (1992) *Decline of Donnish Dominion: The British Academic Professions in the Twentieth Century*. Oxford: Clarendon Press.

Harding, S. (1991) *Whose Science, Whose Knowledge?* Ithaca, NY: Cornell University Press.

Hargreaves, A. (1986) *Two Cultures of Schooling*. London: Falmer Press.

Hargreaves, A. (1994) *Changing Teachers, Changing Times: Teachers' Work and Culture in the Postmodern Age*. New York, NY: Teachers College Press/London: Cassell.

Hargreaves, A. (1996) Revisiting voice, *Educational Researcher*, 25(1): 12–19.

Hargreaves, A. (1998) The emotional practice of teaching, *Teaching and Teacher Education*, 14(8): 835–54.

Hargreaves, A. (1999) Schooling in the new millennium: educational research for the post-modern age, *Discourse: Studies in the Cultural Politics of Education*, 20(3): 333–55.

Hargreaves, A. (2000) Four ages of professionalism and professional learning, *Teachers and Teaching: Theory and Practice*, 6(2): 151–82.

Hargreaves, A. (2001) The emotional geographies of teaching, *Teachers College Record*, 103(6): 1056–80.

Hargreaves, A. and Fullan, M. (1998) *What's Worth Fighting for Out There?*, 2nd edn. New York, NY: Teachers College Press.

Hargreaves, A. and Goodson, I. (1996) Teachers' professional lives: aspirations and actualities, in I. Goodson and A. Hargreaves (eds) *Teachers' Professional Lives*. London: Falmer Press.

Hargreaves, A., Earl, L., Moore, S. and Manning, S. (2001) *Learning to Change: Teaching Beyond Subjects and Standards*. San Francisco, CA: Jossey-Bass.

Harper, K. (2001) Excuses, and cash supply, finally ran out, *Guardian*, 8 October: 10.

Harvey, D. (1989) *The Condition of Postmodernity: An Enquiry into the Origins of Cultural Change*. Oxford: Basil Blackwell.

Hewitt, B. and Fitzsimons, C. (2001) 'I quit', *Guardian Education*, 9 January: 2–3.

Hirst, P. (1989) Implication of government funding policies for research on teaching and teacher education: England and Wales, *Teaching and Teacher Education*, 5(4): 269–81.

Huberman, M. (1993) *The Lives of Teachers*, trans. J. Neufeld. London: Cassell.

Huberman, M. and Miles, M. (1984) *Innovation Up Close*. New York, NY: Plenum.

Huberman, M., Thompson, C. and Weiland, S. (1997) Perspectives on the teaching career, in B. Biddle, T. Good and I. Goodson (eds) *International Handbook of Teachers and Teaching*, 1. London: Kluwer.

Ignatieff, M. (1992) The media admires itself in the mirror, *Observer*, 19 July: 21.

Jameson, F. (1984) Foreword, in J. Lyotard (ed.) *The Postmodern Condition: A Report on Knowledge*. Minneapolis, MN: University of Minnesota Press.

Jeffrey, R. and Woods, P. (1996) Feeling deprofessionalized: the social construction of emotions during an Ofsted inspection, *Cambridge Journal of Education*, 26(3): 325–43.

Kenway, J. (1993) *Economizing Education: The Post-Fordist Directions*. Geelong, Victoria: Deakin University Press.

Klockars, C. (1975) *The Professional Fence*. London: Tavistock.

Knowles, G. and Cole, A. (1991) We're just like those we study – they as beginning teachers, we as beginning professors of teacher education. Letters of the first year. Paper presented to the Thirteenth Conference on Curriculum Theory and Classroom Practice, Bergamo Center, Ohio, October.

Kondratiev, N. (1984) *The Long Wave Cycle*, trans. G. Daniels. New York, NY: Richardson and Snyder.

Kotarbinski, T. (1997) *Dictionary of scientific quotations*, quoted in A. MacKay, *Guardian*, 11 April: 2.

Kridel, C. (ed.) (1998) *Writing Educational Biography: Explorations in Qualitative Research*. New York, NY: Garland.

Lasch, C. (1995) *The Revolt of the Elites and the Betrayal of Democracy*. London: W.W. Norton.

Lawn, M. (1990) From responsibility to competency: a new context for curriculum studies in England and Wales, *Journal of Curriculum Studies*, 22(4): 388–92.

Levinson, D. (1979) *The Seasons of a Man's Life*. New York, NY: Ballantine Books.

Levinson, D. and Levinson, J. (1996) *The Seasons of a Woman's Life*. New York, NY: Alfred A. Knopf.

Lieberman, A. and Grolnick, M. (1998) Educational reform networks: changes in the forms of reform, in A. Hargreaves, A. Lieberman, M. Fullan and D. Hopkins (eds) *International Handbook of Educational Change*, Handbook 5, Vol. 2: 710–29. London: Kluwer.

Liston, D. and Zeichner, K. (1991) *Teacher Education and the Social Conditions of Schooling*. New York, NY: Routledge.

Lortie, D. (1975) *Schoolteacher: A Sociological Study*. Chicago, IL: University of Chicago Press.

Louden, W. (1991) *Understanding Teaching*. London: Cassell.

Lyotard, J. (ed.) (1984) *The Postmodern Condition: A Report on Knowledge*. Minneapolis, MN: University of Minnesota Press.

McClaughlin, M. and Yee, S. (1988) School as a place to have a career, in

A. Lieberman (ed.) *Building a Professional Culture in Schools*. New York, NY: Teachers College Press.

MacDonald, B. (1991) Critical introduction: from innovation to reform – a framework for analysing change, in J. Rudduck (ed.) *Innovation and Change: Developing Involvement and Understanding*. Buckingham: Open University Press.

MacIntyre, A. (1981) *After Virtue: A Study in Moral Theory*. London: Duckworth.

McNeil, L. (2000) *Contradictions of School Reform: Educational Costs of Standardized Testing*. London: RoutledgeFalmer.

Marquand, D. (1988) *The Unprincipled Society*. London: Fontana.

Marquand, D. (1994) There is such a thing as society, *Guardian*, 16 July: 26.

Melly, G. (1993) Look back in angst, *Sunday Times*, 13 June: 9.

Menter, I., Muschamp, Y., Nicholls, P., Ozga, J. and Pollard, A. (1997) *Work and Identity in the Primary School: A Post-Fordist Analysis*. Buckingham: Open University Press.

Meyer, J. and Rowan, B. (1978) The structure of educational organizations, in J. Meyer and W. Marshal *et al.* (eds) *Environments and Organizations: Theoretical and Empirical Perspectives*. San Francisco, CA: Jossey-Bass.

Middleton, S. (1992) Developing a radical pedagogy: autobiography of a New Zealand sociologist of women's education, in I. Goodson (ed.) *Studying Teachers' Lives*. London: Routledge.

Middleton, S. (1993) *Educating Feminists: Life Histories and Pedagogy*. New York, NY: Teachers College Press/London: Sage Publications.

Middleton, S. (1997) *Disciplining Sexuality: Foucault Life Histories and Education*. New York, NY: Teachers College Press.

Mills, C. (1979) *Power, Politics and People*. New York, NY: Oxford University Press.

Moore, S. (1994) Take it slowly from the end, *Guardian*, 17 November: 5.

Morrow, R. and Torres, C. (1999) The state, social movements, and educational reform, in R. Arnove and C. Torres (eds) *Comparative Education: The Dialectic of the Global and the Local*. Lanham: Rowman and Littlefield.

Mulgan, G. and Worpole, K. (1994) Alien life in open space, *Guardian*, 17 November: 24.

Munro, P. (1998) *Subject to Fiction: Women Teachers' Life History Narratives and the Cultural Politics of Resistance*. Buckingham: Open University Press.

Naipaul, V.S. (1988) *The Enigma of Arrival*. London: Penguin.

Nelson, M. (1992) Using oral histories to reconstruct the experiences of women teachers in Vermont, 1900–50, in I. Goodson (ed.) *Studying Teachers' Lives*. London: Routledge.

Newnham, D. (1997) Going loco, *Guardian Weekend*, 1 March: 20–31.

New York Times (1991) Now playing across America: real life, the movie, 20 October: 32.

Passerini, L. (1987) *Fascism in Popular Memory: The Cultural Experience of the Turin Working Class*. Cambridge: Cambridge University Press.

Passerini, L. (1989) Women's personal narratives: myths, experiences and emotions, in Personal Narratives Group (eds) *Interpreting Women's Lives: Feminist Theory and Personal Narratives*. Bloomington, IN: Indiana University Press.

Plummer, K. (2001) *Documents of Life 2: An Invitation to a Critical Humanism*, 2nd edn. London: Sage Publications.

Pollard, A. and Tann, S. (1987) *Reflective Teaching in the Primary School*. London: Cassell.

Popkewitz, T., Tabachnick, R. and Wehlage, G. (1982) *The Myth of Educational Reform: A Study of School Responses to a Program of Educational Change.* Madison, WI: University of Wisconsin Press.

Reid, W. (1984) Curricular topics as institutional categories: Implications for theory and research in the history and sociology of school subjects, in I. Goodson and S. Ball (eds) *Defining the Curriculum: Histories and Ethnographies.* London: Falmer Press.

Reynolds, D., Sullivan, M. and Murgatroyd, S. (1987) *The Comprehensive Experiment*. London: Falmer Press.

Roberts, B. (2002) *Biographical Research*. Buckingham: Open University Press.

Robertson, H-J. (1998) *No More Teachers, No More Books: The Commercialization of Canada's Schools*. Toronto, Ontario: McClelland and Stewart.

Robertson, S. (1994) An exploratory analysis of post-Fordism and teachers' labour, in J. Kenway (ed.) *Economising Education: Post-Fordist Directions*. Geelong: Deakin University Press.

Robertson, S. (1996) Teachers' work, restructuring and post-Fordism: constructing the new professionalism, in I. Goodson and A. Hargreaves (eds) *Teachers' Professional Lives*. London: Falmer Press.

Robertson, S. (1997) Restructuring teachers' labor: 'troubling' post-Fordism, in B. Biddle, T. Good and I. Goodson (eds) *International Handbook of Teachers and Teaching*, 1. London: Kluwer.

Robson, S. (2001) Commentary, *Guardian*, 10 October: 28.

Rosenthal, A. (1992) What's meant and what's mean in the 'family values' battle, *New York Times*, 26 July, sec. 4: 1.

Ross, A. (2001) Heads will roll, *Guardian Education*, 23 January: 8–9.

Russell, T. and Munby, H. (1992) *Teachers and Teaching from Classroom to Reflection*. London: Falmer Press.

Sage, L. (1994) How to do the life: review of C. Brightman's *Writing Dangerously: Mary McCarthy and Her World. The London Review of Books*, 10 February.

Sarason, S. (1996a) *Barometers of Change: Individual, Institutional, Social Transformation.* San Francisco, CA: Jossey-Bass.

Sarason, S. (1996b) *Revisiting the Culture of the School and the Problem of Change.* San Francisco, CA: Jossey-Bass.

Sarason, S. (1998) World War II and schools, in A. Hargreaves, A. Lieberman, M. Fullan and D. Hopkins (eds) *International Handbook of Educational Change*, Handbook 5, Vol. 1: 23–36. London: Kluwer.

Sartre, J. (1961) *Les Chemins de la Liberté* (trilogy translated as *The Age of Reason* [1945]; *The Reprieve* [1947]; *Iron in the Soul* [1949]). London: Penguin.

Schön, D. (1983) *The Reflective Practitioner: How Professionals Think in Action.* New York, NY: Basic Books.

Schools Council (1965) Raising the school leaving age, working paper no. 2, para. 60. London: Schools Council.

Schwab, J. (1978) The practical: a language for curriculum, in I. Westbury and N. Wilkof (eds) *Science, Curriculum and Liberal Education*. Chicago, IL: University of Chicago Press.

Senge, P. (1995) *The Fifth Discipline*. New York, NY: Doubleday.

Sennett, R. (1999) *The Corrosion of Character: The Personal Consequences of Work in the New Capitalism*. London: W.W. Norton.

Sennett, R. and Cobb, J. (1972) *The Hidden Injuries of Class*, 2nd edn. New York, NY: Vintage.

Sheehy, G. (1976) *Passages: Predictable Crises in Adult Life*. New York, NY: Dutton.

Sheehy, G. (1981) *Pathfinders: How to Achieve Happiness by Conquering Life's Crises*. London: Sidgwick and Jackson.

Sheehy, G. (1995) *New Passages: Mapping Your Life Across Time*. Toronto: Random House.

Shils, E. (1972) *The Intellectual and the Powers and other Essays*. Chicago, IL: University of Chicago Press.

Shotter, J. (1993) *Cultural Politics of Everyday Life: Social Constructionism, Rhetoric and Knowing of the Third Kind*. Toronto: University of Toronto Press.

Shrofel, S. (1991) Review essay: school reform, professionalism, and control, *Journal of Educational Thought*, 25(1): 58–70.

Sikes, P., Measor, L. and Woods, P. (1985) *Teachers' Careers: Crises and Continuities*. London: Falmer Press.

Simon, B. (1985) *Does Education Matter?* London: Lawrence and Wishart.

Simon, B. (1990) The National Curriculum, school organisation and the teacher, in J. Rudduck (ed.) *An Education that Empowers: A Collection of Lectures in Memory of Lawrence Stenhouse*. Clevedon: Multilingual Matters.

Simpson, J. (1992) The closing of the American media, *Spectator*, 18 July: 9.

Smith, D. (1987) *The Everyday World as Problematic: A Feminist Sociology*. Boston, MA: Northeaster University Press.

Smith, D. (1990) *Conceptual Practices of Power: A Feminist Sociology of Knowledge*. Toronto: University of Toronto Press.

Steedman, C. (1986) *Landscape for a Good Woman*. London: Virago Press.

Stenhouse, L. (1975) *An Introduction to Curriculum Research and Development*. London: Heinemann.

Stenhouse, L. (1976) Case study as a basis for research in a theoretical contemporary history of education. Mimeo, CARE, University of East Anglia, Norwich.

Taylor, P. (1987) Whiff of defeat in schools scandal, *Times Higher Education Supplement*, 13 November: 14.

Thomas, W. and Znaniecki, F. (1918–1920) *The Polish Peasant in Europe and America*. Chicago, IL: University of Chicago Press.

Thompson, E. (1987) Diary, *London Review of Books*: 21.

Thompson, P. (1988) *The Voices of the Past: Oral History*, 2nd edn. Oxford: Oxford University Press.

Thompson, P., Itzin, C. and Abendstern, M. (1991) *I Don't Feel Old: The Experience of Later Life*, 2nd edn. Oxford: Oxford University Press.

Tierney, W. (1998) Life history's history: subjects foretold, *Qualitative Inquiry*, 4(1): 49–70.

Tierney, W. (2000) Undaunted courage: life history and the postmodern challenge, in N. Denzin and Y. Lincoln (eds) *Handbook of Qualitative Research*, 2nd edn. Thousand Oaks, CA: Sage.

Torres, R. (2000) *One Decade of Education for All: The Challenge Ahead [Una Decada de Educacion para Todos: La Tasrea Pendiente]*. Montevideo: FUM-TEP/ Madrid: Editorial Popular/Caracas: Editorial Laboratorio Educativo/Buenos Aires: IIPE UNESCO/Porto Alegre: Artmed Editoria.

Touraine, A. (1981) *The Voice and the Eye: An Analysis of Social Movements*. Cambridge, MA: Cambridge University Press.

Tripp, D. (1987) Teacher autobiography and classroom practice. Mimeo, Murdoch University, Western Australia.

Tripp, D. (1994) Teachers' lives, critical incidents, and professional practice, *International Journal of Qualitative Studies in Education*, 7(1): 65–76.

Troman, G. (1996) The rise of the new professionals? The restructuring of primary teachers' work and professionalism, *British Journal of Sociology of Education*, 17(4): 473–87.

TTA (Teacher Training Agency) (1998) *Initial Teacher Training Performance Profiles*. London: Teacher Training Agency.

Veblen, T. (1962) *The Higher Learning in America* (reprint of 1918 edn). New York, NY: Hill and Wang.

Webb, R. and Vulliamy, G. (1999) Changing times, changing demands: a comparative analysis of classroom practice in primary schools in England and Finland, *Research Papers in Education*, 14(3): 222–55.

Weiler, K. (1991) Remembering and representing life choices: a critical perspective on teachers' oral history narratives. Mimeo, Tufts University, Medford.

Wells, G. (1986) *The Meaning Makers*. London: Hodder and Stoughton.

Whitty, G. (1997) Marketization, the state, and the re-formation of the teaching profession, in A. Halsey, H. Lauder, P. Brown and A. Wells (eds) *Education: Culture, Economy, and Society*. New York, NY: Oxford University Press.

Williams, R. (1983) Intellectuals behind the scenes, *Times Higher Education Supplement*, 21 January.

Williams, R. (1989) as quoted in *Times Higher Education Supplement*, 29 December: 21.

Willinsky, J. (1989) Getting personal and practical with personal practical knowledge, *Curriculum Inquiry*, 19(3): 247–64.

Wolfe, A. (1989) *Whose Keeper? Social Science and Moral Obligation*. Berkeley, CA: University of California Press.

Wolfe, A. (1996) *Marginalized in the Middle*. Chicago, IL: University of Chicago Press.

Index

LIFE HISTORY RESEARCH IN EDUCATIONAL SETTINGS
LEARNING FROM LIVES

Ivor Goodson and Pat Sikes

It has long been recognized that life history method has a great deal to offer to those engaged in social research. Indeed, right from the start of the twentieth century, eminent sociologists such as W.I. Thomas, C. Wright Mills and Hubert Blumer have suggested that it is the best, the perfect, approach for studying any aspect of social life. In recent years, life history has become increasingly popular with researchers investigating educational topics of all kinds, including: teachers' perceptions and experiences of different areas of their lives and careers; curriculum and subject development; pedagogical practice; and managerial concerns. *Life History Research in Educational Settings* sets out to explore and consider the various reasons for this popularity and makes the case that the approach has a major and unique contribution to make to understandings of schools, schooling and educational experience, however characterized. The book draws extensively on examples of life history research in order to illustrate theoretical, methodological, ethical and practical issues.

Contents
Introduction – Developing life histories – Techniques for doing life history – What have you got when you've got a life story? – Studying teachers life histories and professional practice – Life stories and social context: storylines and scripts – Questions of ethics and power in life history research – Confronting the dilemmas – Bibliography – Index.

144pp   0 335 20713 8 (Paperback)   0 335 20714 6 (Hardback)